One of the greatest challenges for Christ their financial lives in God's hands. In his engaging, candid and relatable manner, Josh Lawson gives us an easy on-ramp onto the highway of God-empowered finances. Prepare to be equipped and blessed!

Robert Herber
Lead Pastor, All Peoples Church, San Diego, CA
Author of *The Partying God*

Over the years we have worked as a team to renovate hundreds of homes that were in pretty bad shape. While those homes needed work both superficially and internally, we have come to see that many peoples' money problems start from the inside out.

Josh has discovered the balance between dealing with the deeper issues of the heart and mind, while also giving practical help.

If you are looking at your financial house and realizing that it needs major help or even a minor repair, then we highly encourage you to read REALIGN and DO WHAT IT SAYS. You won't regret it.

Chip and **Joanna Gaines**
Hosts of popular TV Show

I eagerly read REALIGN: Finding God's Purpose For Your Money because I know and respect the Antioch Community Church culture where Josh Lawson leads. I love Josh's challenge to live into the adventure that Jesus invites all of his followers to experience. His writing encouraged me to respond more fully to Jesus' invitation and listen less to the culture that tells me to prioritize my own comfort and security.

Todd Harper
President, Generous Giving

Imagine feeling perfectly at peace about your finances. It's wonderful to imagine, isn't it? But then comes the crashing reality that we aren't THERE yet.

Josh's book is a powerful reminder that, contrary to popular belief, our financial peace isn't dependent on a destination.

...when I'm debt free

...when I've saved for my kids' college

...when I have a solid retirement account

Instead, financial peace BEGINS the moment we align our hearts with God's purpose.

This book is the complete package. It is a guide for getting our financial life in order SO THAT it can be used not simply for our comfort and security but for the infinitely greater purpose of God's glory.

Kat Lee
Author, InspiredToAction.com

REALIGN is different. It is practical, insightful, and inspiring. Reading REALIGN can help anyone at any stage of life learn to trust God more by addressing financial issues from the inside out.

Josh Lawson inspires the reader to listen to the Lord for all decision-making, but especially in personal finances. Recognizing our attitudes about spending, how they get formed and how to REALIGN them, is the crowning achievement of this book.

Ramiro Peña
Senior Pastor, Christ the King Church
President, Christ the King Ministries International

REALIGN

REALIGN

FINDING GOD'S PURPOSE FOR YOUR MONEY

BY JOSH LAWSON

REALIGN

Published by Clear Day Publishing, a division of Clear Day Media Group LLC, Franklin, TN. cleardaypublishing.com.

Published in association with Lux Creative {theluxcreative.com}

Unless otherwise noted, Scripture quotations are taken from The Holy Bible, New International Version®, NIV® Copyright © 1973, 1978, 1984, 2011 by Biblica, Inc.® Used by permission. All rights reserved worldwide.

Scripture quotations designated NKJV are taken from the New King James Version®. Copyright © 1982 by Thomas Nelson, Inc. Used by permission. All rights reserved.

Scripture quotations designated ESV are taken from The Holy Bible, English Standard Version® (ESV®), copyright © 2001 by Crossway, a publishing ministry of Good News Publishers. Used by permission. All rights reserved.

Scripture quotations designated AMP are taken from the Amplified® Bible, Copyright © 1954, 1958, 1962, 1964, 1965, 1987 by The Lockman Foundation. Used by permission. (www.Lockman.org)

Scripture quotations designated TLB are taken from The Living Bible copyright © 1971. Used by permission of Tyndale House Publishers, Inc., Carol Stream, Illinois 60188. All rights reserved.

ISBN: 978-0-9897277-3-0

Cover Design: Carolynn Seibert {carolynnseibert.com}

Printed in the United States of America.

Library of Congress Control Number: 2014952875

This publication is designed to provide accurate and authoritative information with regard to the subject matter covered. It is sold with the understanding that the publisher is not engaged in rendering legal, accounting, or other professional advice. If legal advice or other expert professional assistance is required, the services of a competent professional person should be sought.

> - From a Declaration of Principles jointly adopted by the Committee of the American Bar Association and a Committee of Publishers and Associations.

This book is dedicated to two special men who
no longer walk among us:

Eric Falk and Mr. Joe Campbell

*Eric, you taught me to love relentlessly and pursue
Jesus above everything else.*

*Mr. Campbell, you believed in me. You called me a leader when I
was a rebel. Even when you had no strength, you gave strength to
the weak, hurting, and forgotten.*

*Your legacies continue to live in my heart, and I pray they will bear
fruit in others. I love you both.*

CONTENTS

FOREWORD

For the last 27 years, I have had the privilege of leading an incredible group of people we call Antioch Community Church. When we began the ministry, it was our desire to live out the New Testament, just as we read about in the Bible. We wanted to be people who weren't just hearers of the Word, but doers of the Word. We were committed to prayer, sharing our faith, discipleship, and reading the Bible and applying its truth to our lives.

We realized that if we were going to see people live radical lives for Jesus we would have to deal with the issues of money and possessions. When I look back at my years of church planting and church impact in our city, nation, and around the world, I cannot overstate the importance of dealing with the issue of money. Only when we set our hearts straight and align ourselves with doing it God's way, instead of our own, can we fully embrace His purposes for our lives.

When Josh first came to me and shared his heart for helping people in the church neighborhood (one of the poorest zip codes in Texas) who struggled with finances we said, "Absolutely, we are with you. The only problem is we don't have any money to fund that particular ministry." How ironic. But, as God would have it, Josh said, "I believe so much in it that Jenny and I will live by faith. We will sacrifice, even financially, to see others set free." And that is exactly what they have done. Josh began to facilitate an existing financial program on Sundays. During the first three years we saw more than three million dollars of debt eliminated, we saw people personally set free, marriages restored and healed, and miracles began to happen in the context of community. It was during this time that Josh began to develop his own curriculum with heaven and eternity as the foundation and where radical giving became more important than creating wealth and stability. So Josh and Jenny began to look at their lives, their friends' lives and our experiences as a church community to shape and form what you are now about to experience through their new book, REALIGN.

I am so excited about this book and the curriculum. It provides very concrete and practical ideas/instruction/coaching so people can build their lives around Jesus and His purposes and not just self-interest. When that happens at a financial level, it will happen at every other level, and we will see the Kingdom of God made real. Until we touch the area of finances, our hearts will always be divided. But when we transform the area of finance, then people are set free to do anything that God would have them do in any area of the world.

This book is not just a recounting of principles, but evidence and fruit of a life well-lived by Josh and Jenny Lawson, their family and a community of people who have lived this out the last three decades. Enjoy! It will be life changing.

Jimmy Seibert

Pastor, Antioch Community Church, Waco, Texas
President, Antioch Ministries International

INTRODUCTION

REALIGN

FELLOWSHIP OF THE BROKEN

Stephanie had hit rock bottom. As she drove away from the house, a sudden realization came to her – she had just lost everything in life that mattered. Her lifestyle choices had finally compelled her to take the kids, deserting her husband, and move to the other side of town. One following Sunday, a friend invited her to church. Stephanie knew her life needed to change but thought church was for people who had if all figured out, and she knew she was nowhere near perfect. The first day at church Stephanie heard the good news that Jesus loved her and came to take her sin away. She was overwhelmed to now have a relationship with God ... and relieved she didn't have to be perfect!

Over the next several months, Stephanie continued to attend church and applied what she was hearing. Each week, as Stephanie connected with others, she realized her struggles, though painful, were not unique, and God wanted to transform every area of her life.

In time, the relationships with her husband and kids improved and eventually they moved back in together. Her husband could see something was different about her, so one Sunday morning he decided to check out her church. That morning they noticed an announcement in the bulletin for a financial class being held at the church.

During their separation, they had accumulated an incredible amount of debt. In addition to car notes and student loans, together they tallied up $65,500 in credit card debt. The mountain of debt seemed impossible to overcome with their level of income, but after attending the class, they committed to no longer bend to cultural pressures and decided to align their finances with God's ways.

Over the next several months, they made incredible strides paying down their debt, but the journey would not be easy. A few months into the process, Stephanie's husband was let go from his job. He finally landed another, but within a matter of months was in search mode again. It seemed that no matter how badly they wanted to get their lives back in order, they just couldn't get a break.

However, over the following months and years, they stuck to their commitment, keeping God in the center of their finances. Their dream of financial freedom was finally reached, when after four and a half years, they paid off the last credit card!

When I asked Stephanie how she felt, she exclaimed, "It's like I had one of those dog choke collars around my neck for so many years. I couldn't do anything because there was something constantly pulling me back, and with each pull would come deep agony. But as soon as we paid off our last debt, it was as though God came down and took that collar off! I feel like I can breathe and live again."

BROKENNESS ABOUNDS

If we were honest, we would probably admit there is a piece of Stephanie's story that resounds inside each of us. Maybe financially or relationally our situation isn't as dire, but all of us are broken to a certain degree. And this brokenness affects every area of our lives, but we are not alone.

Whenever I teach our *REALIGN* financial classes, my favorite week is the first one. During the discussion time, we have each person share why they are in the class. Normally the answers begin with surface-level confessions as people admit they are "a little stressed" or they "just want to know what God has to say about money." But as the discussion evolves and people get more comfortable and vulnerable, they begin to share the true reasons. A person who looks like he has it all together shares how he has contemplated divorcing his wife because their money fights never end. The businessman with the expensive suit admits he's in debt up to his eyeballs and can't sleep because bankruptcy looms in the near future. A single mom shares her story of never having quite enough to make ends meet and feels like she is on the edge of spiraling out of control. Recent college graduates open up about their fear of the future and the unrelenting pressure to become "financially successful" when they don't even know where to begin.

Everyone has a story, and if we peel back the surface-level problems of debt, anxiety, and money fights, we'd realize there is more brokenness than we would like to admit or probably even realize.

Maybe this all sounds familiar. Perhaps you aren't really sure there is enough to make it until the next paycheck, let alone to pay the mortgage. Or, maybe you find yourself trapped in an ever-escalating façade, requiring more and more spending to maintain appearances. And you are desperately afraid that you will be exposed as a fraud. If you're like me, you may think about your bank account more than you'd like to admit.

Well, if any of this is you, welcome to the "fellowship of the broken." We all have our shortcomings, stories and screw-ups. No one has it all figured out. Honestly, the ones who look like they have it all figured out were probably in my office last week telling me how they DON'T have it all figured out! You are not alone in your insecurity, hopelessness, and frustration.

GOD'S ORIGINAL PURPOSE

So how did we get to this place of such brokenness? And is there a better way? In order to make sense of our mess and understand how to fix it, we need to start at the beginning ... the very beginning! When we look at the Garden of Eden, we find God's original purpose for our lives. We see that the primary relationship between man and God was built on trust.

WELCOME TO THE "FELLOWSHIP OF THE BROKEN." WE ALL HAVE OUR SHORTCOMINGS, STORIES AND SCREW-UPS. NO ONE HAS IT ALL FIGURED OUT.

BROKEN RELATIONSHIPS

In Genesis 3:1-3 we read where Satan shows up to destroy Eve's trust in God. He cunningly said to the woman, "Did God really say, 'You must not eat from any tree in the garden'?" Satan intended to create doubt in Eve's mind and cause them eternal separation.

Ultimately, Eve bought the lie, trust was broken, and sin entered the world. Adam and Eve now hid from Him because they were ashamed. Adam said in Genesis 3:10, "I heard you in the garden, and I was afraid because I was naked; so I hid." This fundamentally brought turmoil and conflict – with one another, within themselves and with all creation. The very foundation of their lives was unstable and misaligned.

Further, we see that sin affected Adam and Eve's relationship with one another. They began to blame each other for what happened: "The man said, 'The woman you put here with me – she gave me some fruit from the tree, and I ate it.'"[1] Their once peaceful relationship was now broken.

BROKEN COVERINGS

Many teachings about original sin stop at describing how sin caused brokenness in our relationship with God, but fail to include the damage inflicted on our management of God's resources.

Realizing they were naked, Adam and Eve "sewed fig leaves together and made coverings for themselves,"[2] in an attempt to cover their shame. They used what God had created (fig leaves) in a way God did not intend. God knew their coverings were insufficient, so He "made garments of skin for Adam and his wife and clothed them."[3]

In the same way that Adam and Eve used fig leaves as an inadequate covering, we attempt to hide our shame and insecurity by covering ourselves with material possessions. We believe we have to get stuff to cover it up, or we swing to the other side and embrace our sin as our identity.

The original act of sin caused brokenness to ripple throughout eternity and into every area of human existence, even into our resources. Romans 5:12 explains what happened: "Therefore, just as sin entered the world through one man, and death [brokenness] through sin, and in this way death [brokenness] came to all people, because all sinned." And we still suffer the consequences to this day.

GOOD NEWS

But there is good news! God, in His kindness and great mercy offers us redemption through the broken body of His son Jesus. The Bible paints a beautiful picture of the transformation that happened when Jesus gave His life for us. The book of Romans says, "Consequently, just as one trespass [eating the fruit] resulted in condemnation for all people so also one righteous act [Jesus dying on the cross] resulted in justification and life for all people."[4]

5

Through Jesus, not only do we have assurance of salvation, but we are also invited to allow His transformational power into every area of our lives. We can have restored identities, relationships, and a renewed purpose for our money, as we realign with His way of doing things.

Paul tells us in Ephesians 4 how this takes place: "You were taught, with regard to your former way of life, to put off your old self, which is being corrupted by its deceitful desires; to be made new in the attitude of your minds; and to put on the new self, created to be like God in true righteousness and holiness."[5] This same transformation will affect our financial lives both inside and out, as we believe God's truth and operate according to His purposes.

IN THE SAME WAY THAT ADAM AND EVE USED FIG LEAVES AS AN INADEQUATE COVERING, WE ATTEMPT TO HIDE OUR SHAME AND INSECURITY BY COVERING OURSELVES WITH MATERIAL POSSESSIONS.

LADDER ON THE RIGHT WALL

Understanding how we currently make financial decisions is the first step in realigning our finances with God's purposes. We must recognize and acknowledge what influences have shaped our beliefs and governed our actions.

In his book, *The 7 Habits of Highly Effective People*, Stephen R. Covey encourages the reader to "start with the end in mind."[6] It is a simple strategy of asking ourselves where we want to end up and then aligning our lives and behaviors to get us there. Every day of our lives we are taking steps, whether knowingly or unknowingly, in a particular direction. The question then becomes which direction are we going? Covey writes about making sure to place the ladder, which we are climbing, on the right wall.

Many financial teachings today place the ladder on the wrong wall. Too often, they may teach biblical principles, but without a clear call to live for God's Kingdom. Teaching principle-centered financial living will only lead to behavior modification, with our dreams and our goals as the target, rather than change from the inside. This was never God's intention for our financial lives. It is actually similar to the condemnation Jesus gives to the Pharisees, "Woe to you, teachers of the law and Pharisees, you hypocrites! You clean the outside of the cup and dish, but inside they are full of greed and self-indulgence. Blind Pharisee! First clean the inside of the cup and dish, and then the outside also will be clean."[7]

Jesus is concerned about the whole person and does not wish for us to live by outward appearances while being corrupt and unclean on the inside. His desire is for us to make financial decisions that are integrated with a daily relationship with Him – not simply by following a set of rules and laws. This requires our willingness to change from the inside-out. As we place Jesus at the center of our financial lives and decisions, we are affirming our relationship with Him and our decisions then become more about what we can do to advance His Kingdom and His glory here on the earth. This is God's purpose for our finances – to know Him and make Him known.

COMFORT IS KING

All too often financial teachings and our personal financial goals communicate that the ultimate objective is to have enough resources to do whatever you want to do, whether it's to buy a bigger house, a luxury car, or have a nice nest egg set aside for retirement. Rather than focusing on building the Kingdom of God, we are seeking self-gratification and security in our finances.

We believe if we can control our finances and save enough money to create a little buffer zone of comfort, then we can avoid much of the pain life brings. From that place of self-sufficiency and independence, we end up saying "yes" to whatever is easy and "no" to things that might get us out of our comfort zone. Instead of saying "yes" to the great adventures God is calling us to, we end up settling for second best. One of my biggest reasons for writing this book is my concern that we are becoming people who live "good Christian lives." We don't sin too much and appear acceptable and good, but we order our lives so there is no need to trust God because we have it all together.

COMPARISON KILLS

If our own self-generated desire for comfort and security wasn't enough, we are bombarded with messages on television, radio, and the internet telling us which cars to buy, what fashions to wear, what investments to make ... and on and on. We are enthralled by how much celebrities, sports figures, and business leaders are making. We have been sucked into the undercurrent of culture, which tells us life is all about how much money we have in the bank, how big our house is, how significant our job title sounds, and how much financial independence we have attained. As a result, we align our lives with what culture and this world define as desirable and successful. And it is killing us! We are working longer hours and spending more money than ever, but we can't ever seem to catch up to where we *should* be.

> **AS WE PLACE JESUS AT THE CENTER OF OUR FINANCIAL LIVES AND DECISIONS, WE ARE AFFIRMING OUR RELATIONSHIP WITH HIM AND OUR DECISIONS THEN BECOME MORE ABOUT WHAT WE CAN DO TO ADVANCE HIS KINGDOM AND HIS GLORY HERE ON THE EARTH.**

SHATTERED DREAM

Thankfully, for me, my dream of comfort and security was shattered early on. When we first launched our ministry, I was invited to a fundraising event in Dallas, so I went as a learning experience. It quickly became apparent I was the youngest in the room, by several decades, and clearly the poorest by a few million. I sat around a table with a group of grey-haired men and women, all who had reached the pinnacles of success in their respective industries.

During one of the discussion times, the man to my right, whose wardrobe cost more than my car, began to open up to the group. With a glassy look in his eyes, he recounted how he had worked his entire life to get where he was. The previous week he had closed a billion dollar deal (that's billion with a "B") and he owned the nicest houses and drove the nicest cars, but he paused, folded his hands for a few seconds, then looked around the table. With a deep sense of sobriety, he admitted, "I thought that once I reached this point I would be happy. But I am now standing on top of a mountain and have everything I could want in the world, but I'm miserable." He had climbed that ladder all the way to the top only to find it was leaning on the wrong wall.

Sadly, his story is not unusual. I have met with countless individuals who look successful on the outside and seem to have it all together, but admit their lives have no purpose and their wealth cannot quench the misery in their hearts. They had aligned their lives with a false hope ... that money or riches would satisfy. Their ladders were placed on the wrong wall, and regretfully, they are just now figuring it out.

But your story can be different. You can choose to *REALIGN* your life and finances with God's purpose and you can find true peace and hope. For some of you it might take a major shift. For others, it might just be a slight tweak here and there. On whichever wall your ladder is leaning, let me just suggest, it's not too late – change is possible.

REALIGNING TO WHAT?

In Matthew 6:31-32, Jesus tells His followers how to handle the stress of finances. He says, "Therefore do not worry, saying, 'What shall we eat?' or 'What shall we drink?' or 'What shall we wear?' For after all these things the Gentiles seek. For your heavenly Father knows that you need all these things" (NKJV). So then, Jesus is contrasting two differing attitudes toward our basic needs. In verse 32 (above) He says, "... all these things the Gentiles seek." Believers too, were influenced by popular culture and making decisions based solely on what they wanted to eat, drink, and wear. Sounds a lot like us today, doesn't it?

But in the next verse Jesus tells us how we, as believers, should handle these concerns, "But seek first the Kingdom of God and His righteousness, and all these things shall be added to you."[8] He is inviting us to trust God to provide. "Don't worry," Jesus says. Lift up your eyes from the material things of this world and realign your life with the Kingdom of God and His way of doing things.

This is step number one for all of you note-takers out there. Put God's Kingdom first, and only when we do that will we have true peace and purpose with our money. Seems contradictory not to worry, but when we put His Kingdom first, everything else – your work, your relationships, and your future – will make more sense.

> **LIFT UP YOUR EYES FROM THE MATERIAL THINGS OF THIS WORLD AND REALIGN YOUR LIFE WITH THE KINGDOM OF GOD AND HIS WAY OF DOING THINGS.**

HAPPY OR HOLY?

When Jenny and I were first engaged, I was given a book called *Sacred Marriage* by Gary Thomas.[9] I let it sit on my shelf for a few months, but after we got into a nice, heated "discussion" I decided it was finally time to open the book. After reading only a few pages, I was put squarely in my place. The premise of the book is this: "What if God designed marriage to make us holy more than to make us happy?" After years of believing that God would give me a spouse to make life happier, I suddenly realized marriage is about making me more like Him. Talk about pulling the rug out from under me, I'm glad I read the book when I did! It challenged me to set my ladder on the right wall and love my wife, as I should.

The same is true for our financial lives. If we believe that God has given us money to make us happy and comfortable, then we are probably going to handle our resources in the same way. However, if we understand that God's purpose for our money is to know Him and make Him known, then it alters how we manage our resources on a day-to-day basis.

WHOSE DREAMS ARE THEY ANYWAY?

Throughout the Bible we see where God has given great dreams to His people. Whether it was Noah building the ark, Nehemiah rebuilding the wall around Jerusalem, or Abraham becoming the Father of a great nation, He has consistently given His people visions that were bigger than anything they could have thought possible.

Many times these "dreams" of God's didn't exactly match up with what they had envisioned for themselves. When God called Abraham, it was mixed with both sacrifice and promise. Genesis 12 says, "The LORD had said to Abram, 'Go from your country, your people and your father's household to the land I will show you. I will make you into a great nation, and I will bless you; I will make your name great, and you will be a blessing. I will bless those who bless you, and whoever curses you I will curse; and all peoples on earth will be blessed through you.'"[10] Wow! What an incredible promise! But also, what a demanding sacrifice! Abraham was riding away into the sunset … he was ready to relax in his remaining years. After all, he was seventy-five years old and was set for life. But God had other ideas and invited him to give up his plans and go on an adventure with Him.

I believe God has either already planted or wants to plant adventurous dreams inside each of us – dreams to have an impact and to change the world – things like ending world hunger and putting a stop to sex trafficking, or perhaps building orphanages in Africa, or giving away millions to fund indigenous businesses. These are big, God-sized, dreams! But here's the kicker, in order to see these things accomplished, we must *REALIGN* our lives with God's way of doing things. Our prayer must become, "Father ... your kingdom come, your will be done, on earth as it is in heaven."[11] This could mean giving up another, more personal, dream, but whenever we offer our desires as a sacrifice, there are two things that can happen: God will either replace it with something better or He will purify it so that it isn't about our kingdom but His.

Whenever God gives us these big dreams, I believe He will also provide all the resources we need to accomplish them. With Noah, God gave him clear directions on how to build the ark. With Nehemiah, God changed the heart of the king and provided everything he needed to see the walls rebuilt. And with Abraham, God led him and his family and provided for them every step of the way.

For some of you, maybe most, considering such grand dreams is more than you can even think about. Life is too overwhelming and you just want to know how to pay your rent. Let me encourage you that we will get you there, and when we talk about "dreams" it can also mean normal things like paying your debts off and making ends meet. However, the key is to understand that even though you have all the practical concerns to take care of, God still wants to partner with you to unleash your resources for a greater purpose – His purpose. Our job is to pray, "God, if you have dreams you want to see accomplished, dream them through me. And help me align my resources so that those dreams are accomplished."

WHAT'S NEXT?

In the next several chapters I will show you how to accomplish God's purpose for your money by realigning three key areas of your financial life: **Beliefs, Plans, and Focus**.

We will start at the foundational level of what it means to *REALIGN YOUR BELIEFS*. The financial choices we make and the actions we take are directly impacted by what we believe. Therefore we have to realign what we believe about God, ourselves, and money, with God's truth.

Next we will discuss, from a practical perspective, how to *REALIGN YOUR PLANS* and manage your financial life. In the Garden of Eden we see that God partnered with Adam and Eve as His managers. Their duty was to tend the garden and bring forth a harvest. In this section, I will show you what God's expectations are for you as His manager and how you can realign your resources with His original intentions.

And finally, we will discuss how to *REALIGN YOUR FOCUS*. You can have the greatest beliefs and plans, but if you do not remain focused, then it is all for naught. Focus is the glue that holds your entire plan together and ensures that you stay on track for the long haul. Finishing with a "capstone course", a summary of all that you've learned, you will be challenged to impact the world with your resources – generously giving in ways you never imagined possible.

After each chapter, I will give you some application questions to help you process what we you are reading. I encourage you to go through this book with at least one other person. Whether you are single or married, the important thing is to find someone who can hold you accountable to implement what you read.

For my wife Jenny, and me, finance is a tough subject for us to talk through. We have had a lot of challenges learning how to get on the same page. Yet, as we have spent literally hundreds of hours listening to one another and processing through books and teachings, it has brought healing and deeper intimacy to our relationship. I believe the same thing can happen in your life and that is why we are passionate about this subject.

Above all, I want you to bring God into the process. My simple hope and prayer is by reading this book, you will desire a closer walk with God.

GOD STILL WANTS TO PARTNER WITH YOU TO UNLEASH YOUR RESOURCES FOR A GREATER PURPOSE – HIS PURPOSE.

PART ONE

REALIGN
YOUR
BELIEFS

ROOTS BEFORE FRUITS

While a senior in high school, I became extremely insecure about one of my teeth because it was noticeably smaller than the rest. My dentist did an X-ray and found it was, in fact, a baby tooth and had not developed a permanent tooth above it. He decided to give me a crown and it worked out quite nicely for several years.

One night I was eating at a Mexican restaurant with my family, bit down on a chip and felt a piece of my fake tooth break off. As I rubbed my tongue along the back of the tooth, I could feel a crack right down the center. The next day, I went back to my dentist and he put a brand new, temporary crown on it. He told me it was only a short-term solution and would eventually need to be replaced with an implant. He also said that since it was a baby tooth, it would sooner or later fall out.

Over the next two years, that brand-new, white crown slowly changed colors – getting darker and darker. I would have nightmares about biting into a piece of pizza or an apple and leaving my tooth behind. Finally one day, the tooth became too dark for my gracious wife to bear any longer, so she told me it was time to get my "nasty" tooth checked out.

I visited my dentist and presented my belief that simply drinking too much coffee had caused the outside of my tooth to darken.

But after a few minutes of working hard to take the fake tooth off, he offered me a mirror so I could see what my tooth looked like. I grabbed the mirror expecting to see my cute, little, white baby tooth shining back at me, but instead what greeted me was a nasty, black bony structure, which would have worked nicely as one of Gollum's teeth in *The Lord of the Rings*!

My dentist informed me the real reason my tooth was darkening over time was because my baby tooth was slowly rotting from the inside out because it had weak roots.

The procedure to fix the problem was a simple, one-day surgery and after a few months of healing, they would insert a new, permanent tooth. Obviously, it's a costly procedure that takes more time and effort than I wanted to give, but it would permanently solve the problem.

DEEPER PROBLEMS

My black tooth issue is similar to many of our financial problems. We ultimately cannot get away from what is on the inside. We can keep on making the "quick and easy fixes," but we will eventually have to face the music and deal with the root cause. What I have found from years of experience, is that below the surface of our financial problems are deeper issues caused by our beliefs (weak roots).

Science has actually proven that whatever we regularly think about will eventually come out in our actions. I guarantee that the majority of our financial brokenness is caused by broken beliefs. However, properly aligned beliefs will always help us rightly manage our finances towards accomplishing God's purposes. The foremost step in realigning our financial lives is to realign our beliefs. In order to get this done, we must first understand the root of the issues – where our beliefs come from.

WHERE DO BELIEFS COME FROM?

Noted psychologist Erik Erikson, in his theory on psychosocial development, says trust is the foundational developmental task for human beings.[1] As a child, when we first come out of the womb, one of our primary needs is to trust (normally we trust our mom). As we move through the developmental years, we begin to trust other people, experiences, and thoughts, which in turn form our beliefs about the world around us. Therefore, beliefs are the lenses through which we see and understand life. They are continually re-shaped by the actions of others, events in our lives, cultural pressures, and more than anything, our thought life and how we process information. What you believe about yourself and the world around you determines how you will interact with your money. You may not realize it, but what you believe about yourself, God, and money is already manifested in your actions. In *figure 1*, we can see a simple explanation of this process. Trust is the foundational center of our lives, and from this core, we develop our beliefs about the world around us and from which our actions (fruits) flow.

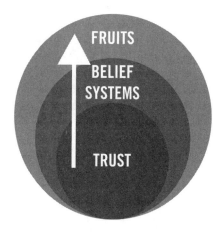

figure 1

TRULY

I have some dear friends who decided to adopt a precious little girl from China; they named her Truly. Within a few short days of having her home, they noticed she had some unusual eating tendencies. During mealtime, she would become extremely nervous and anxious. My friends would place food on her plate, where upon she would quickly grab all of the food she could and stuff her mouth. This continued for some time with every single meal.

My friends asked their adoption specialist about it and were told, "More than likely, Truly had been in an orphanage where she was not given an adequate amount of food, and meals were skipped." This caused Truly to develop a deep distrust that she would be provided food, so when mealtime came she believed she had to get her food quickly and store it in her cheeks because the next meal was uncertain.

BELOW THE SURFACE OF OUR FINANCIAL PROBLEMS, THERE IS ALWAYS A DEEPER ISSUE CAUSED BY OUR BELIEFS.

Her broken trust, from past experience, led to broken beliefs, which in turn led her to act out in anxiety and fear. Her previously learned beliefs were driving her current actions. Even though she was in a new family, where she had unlimited love, support and food, she still operated under her old, broken beliefs.

Over the next several months, my friends would continue to affirm their love for Truly, assuring her that she was secure and would get all the food she needed. As Truly's trust was established, her beliefs were transformed, which led to more appropriate actions and happier meal times!

GETTING TO THE ROOTS

Imagine a massive oak tree, in your mind, with branches stretching out dozens of feet. How does a massive oak tree like that get nutrients to its leaves and fruit? I'm not an arborist, but if my memory of third grade ecology class serves me correctly, it comes from the roots.

Whatever is going on below the surface of that tree will eventually make its way to the branches, leaves, and fruit. Our beliefs are similar to the roots of that enormous oak tree. Each of us has a "root system" that feeds the fruit in every area of our life – in work, in finances, in friendships, etc. Whatever is fed to those roots, will eventually flow into the fruit. The ultimate health of our lives and finances is directly linked to the health of our root systems – our beliefs.

The Bible tells us that our minds produce two very distinct types of fruit, with polar opposite results. Romans 8:5-6 says, "Those who live according to the flesh have their minds set on what the flesh desires; but those who live in accordance with the Spirit have their minds set on what the Spirit desires. The mind governed by the flesh is death, but the mind governed by the Spirit is life and peace."

Jesus reiterates this point when He says, "By their fruit you will recognize them. Do people pick grapes from thornbushes, or figs from thistles? Likewise every good tree bears good fruit, but a bad tree bears bad fruit. A good tree cannot bear bad fruit, and a bad tree cannot bear good fruit."[2]

You can spend all of your time and energy trying to "pluck bad fruit," but if you want to have healthy fruit in your life, you must address the unhealthy beliefs festering beneath the surface. In order to have lasting change, addressing the roots before the fruits, is essential.

If you desire to change how you think, then you must change what you believe. Changing what you believe is no easy task, but it will only come when you alter where and in whom you place your trust.

IN ORDER TO HAVE LASTING CHANGE, ADDRESSING THE ROOTS BEFORE THE FRUITS, IS ESSENTIAL.

APPLICATION QUESTIONS

In what ways have you tried to "mask" your problems instead of dealing with the deeper issues?

Take a minute and reflect on how you see the world around you. How do your beliefs shape your daily actions?

In what ways have your beliefs formed healthy actions/behaviors in your life? What about unhealthy actions?

Consider the oak tree analogy – what are you feeding your roots?

LIES THAT DRIVE

Satan is the master at playing head games with us. That's why the Bible calls him the father of lies. He relentlessly deceives us, again and again and again. His main purpose in this world is to steal, kill, and destroy, and his method of accomplishing this is by deceiving us with his lies. If he can get us to trust the lies he's feeding us, he knows it will radically change the way we see the world around us and alter our decisions.

ROOTED IN LIES

Lies are constantly being fed to us, day in and day out, and more often than not, we don't even realize we're listening to them. Usually it will come across as a simple, innocent thought such as, "I'm just bad with money." Or, "I'll always be in debt." Perhaps you tell yourself something like, "I'll never be as successful as so-and-so." And it might *feel* very true. You might not be a financial whiz and find it challenging to consistently stay on a budget, but putting your trust in a lie is not the solution. Acknowledging these beliefs about you will eventually take root and lead to misguided actions. It actually becomes a self-fulfilling prophecy, as you will choose either not to care, treating money carelessly, or move to the opposite end of the spectrum, attempting to control it out of fear and insecurity.

YOU ARE NOT THE ONLY ONE

One of the more common lies Satan feeds us is a variation of "you are the only one." He will subtly attack us with these thoughts as he whispers to us, "You're the only one who is dealing with this." "No one else feels what you're feeling." "You can't tell anyone because they'll think you are such a terrible person." "You can't go to that financial class because you're the only one with this issue." He feeds us these lies until we cower in shame and pull away from God's people and purposes.

When I was a senior in high school, I believed the lie that I was the odd-man-out and everyone else had his or her act together. I was already fairly insecure, but during the fall of that year several events happened that caused me to become even more uncertain. I would come home every day from school and sulk in my room for hours believing that no one understood me. I felt so weird and out of place. I honestly believed God had made a mistake when He made me.

On the outside though, no one could tell. It looked like I had it all together. I was still doing great in sports and had plenty of friends. As I continued to believe the lies, I began to pull away from people. For several months I would sit in the dark each night and think about what the world would be like without me. I kept sinking deeper and deeper until one night I finally decided that I was done being "the only one."

I began writing a note to my parents, telling them how sorry I was for what I was about to do. "I just wasn't meant to be here. I am the only one on earth who is struggling, and everyone else has it figured out."

Several minutes later my mom walked into the room. Sensing that something was wrong, she sat down beside me. I tried to explain what was going on with me, but I just couldn't get it out. She was having a hard time understanding. I eventually became frustrated and asked her to leave me alone. But with tears in her eyes she said, "Joshua, I am not leaving your side. I've been through this with both of your brothers, and I went through this with all three of my brothers. You are not the only one to ever feel this way."

She then proceeded to tell me that many young men go through those same feelings at about my age. As she spoke, I could feel myself whispering, "Really?" I had felt so alone for so many months. I had believed lie after lie from the enemy. And believing those lies almost cost me my life.

UNRELENTING RECORDING

Whenever we teach our *REALIGN* financial class, we ask our class members to spend a few minutes and think about the various thoughts that go through their minds during the course of the day. People are amazed by how many lies they believe on a consistent basis. Normally, we listen to the same lies over and over, like a perpetual recording playing in the background. We just don't take the time to hit pause and consider them. If we could somehow find the will to stop the repeating refrain, we would discover that most of what we hear is either negative or destructive.

OUR DAILY THOUGHTS DETERMINE THE SUBSTANCE OF WHO WE ARE AND EVENTUALLY ... OUR ACTIONS.

One day I was meeting with a couple that was in a pretty desperate place. They had accumulated a lot of debt, and both were constantly stressed about their bills and lack of money. Month in, month out, they were running hard on the proverbial hamster wheel, trying to play catch-up with ever-increasing bills and overdue payments. I could tell there was a little bit more going on "below the surface," so I asked the husband, "Hey man, whenever you think about money and think about yourself, what's the first thought that comes to mind?"

He stared blankly at the ground and I could tell he was trying to listen to the thoughts inside his head. Then, after several seconds of silence, he replied, "Honestly? What I hear is that all this is my fault because I'm just not smart enough to figure it out. I'm ruining my family's life. I'm a failure." He put his face in his hands and began to weep. "God is mad at me. I try to pray, but I think God won't listen to me because of my financial mess."

I looked at him and said, "That's not what God thinks about you. Why don't we take a minute and ask God what is true?"

He obliged and muttered out a simple prayer, "God, what is true?" We sat there quietly. After several minutes the silence was broken; he began weeping uncontrollably, crying out, "He's proud of me. He's proud of me! God told me He's proud of me, and is going to help us out of this!"

My friend had been living in a cesspool of toxic thinking. The lies that he believed were infecting every area of his life. He believed he was so bad that God wouldn't listen to him, so he stopped praying. He believed that he couldn't get his family back on track financially, so he gave his wife the task of trying to figure things out. He believed that he was a failure, so he became distant from his friends and family.

Proverbs 23:7 says, "As he thinks within himself, so he is" (NASB). Our daily thoughts determine the substance of who we are and eventually ... our actions. For my friend, the lies he believed became his reality.

Whether we realize it or not, each of us is daily attacked with a barrage of lies. Satan does not want us to become the people that God intends, so he will do everything in his power to keep us believing his lies. He doesn't play nicely, and he is playing for keeps. Remember, Satan's goal is to "steal, kill, and destroy" you. Awareness of the enemy's tactics is the first step toward freedom.

Read through the list and consider if you have ever believed one or more of these lies. Put a check next to those you listen to on a consistent basis.

EXAMPLES OF LIES WE BELIEVE

_____ I am bad at managing money

_____ I am worthless and not good enough

_____ I will always be poor

_____ God will provide for my needs, but is annoyed by my wants

_____ I have to earn the right to prosper with money

_____ Money and things are evil and divert me from the Kingdom

_____ I will eventually lose everything I have

_____ I will always have to take care of myself

_____ I will never be as wealthy or successful as _____

_____ I am a bad Christian because I have money

_____ God only wants me in church to give to His purposes

_____ I am just stupid

_____ I could never tell others how much I make

_____ I have earned this money and deserve to spend it as I want

_____ I don't have enough money to give

Adapted from Stephen DeSilva[1.]

FLEXIBLE BRAINS

After reflecting on your response to the list of lies, you might be thinking you will never be able to win the battle for your mind, that it's way too difficult. This itself is a very BIG lie! The brain is a beautiful creation, and one of the most incredible facts about the brain is that it is extremely flexible and can be changed.[2] Even if you have developed deep-seeded habits of believing or acting in certain ways, you can literally change the brain's chemical make-up with thoughts and behavior. But this can only happen over time, as you daily practice new habits of replacing lies with truth.

> YOUR MIND IS NOT UNCHANGEABLE
> AND CAN LITERALLY BE MADE NEW AND REALIGNED,
> THE WAY GOD INTENDS.

CHANGED BELIEFS

So how do you change your beliefs? You have to replace those lies with truths. Simple enough, but it will take time and effort. Just imagine yourself paving a new information highway in your brain, one that truth travels instead of lies. It will not be rebuilt overnight, but stick with it and you will soon begin to see change in your daily habits and actions.

In his letter to the Roman church, Paul encourages them, "Do not be conformed to the pattern of this world, but be transformed by the renewing of your mind."[3] Do you want to be transformed? Do you want to get out of debt? Stay out of debt? Are you tired of always feeling like a loser with your money? Do you want to give more? So then, transformation will come "by the renewing of your mind." Your mind is not unchangeable and can literally be made new and realigned, the way God intends. For years I have taught people (in our classes) three easy-to-remember steps to fight the barrage of lies. Just remember these words ... **Stop It, Switch It, Speak It.**

STOP IT

The word "repent," means to change your way of thinking. It doesn't just mean to say, "I'm sorry," or to have some vague sense of regret and remorse, but instead is an intentional turning away from something towards something better. If God is showing you that you consistently believe the lie that you will always be poor and never have enough, He's bringing this to your attention for a purpose. This is the first step – your moment to **Stop It**.

As soon as you hear a lie in your mind, act forcefully with intentionality to stop it and replace it with truth. Don't let it take root. In 2 Corinthians 10:5 Paul encourages believers to be forceful dealing with their thought life. He says, "We demolish arguments and every pretension that sets itself up against the knowledge of God, and we take captive every thought to make it obedient to Christ." We have to realize we are always at war in our minds and we are either winning the battle or losing it – there's no middle ground! To consistently have victory we must fight like we mean it, with our hearts and desires fully engaged. How badly do you want it?

Changing your daily thoughts will require radical steps. Prominent psychologist, Dr. Henry Cloud, says that ninety percent of the thoughts we had yesterday, we will have again today.[4]

So, if a good share of the thoughts you had yesterday were based on lies, then those same thoughts are going to naturally be going through your mind again today! You will not change your thoughts by passively hoping they get better on their own. You must intentionally put in the time and effort to stop those old lies from taking root and redirect them to something new.

> WHEN OUR BELIEFS ARE
> GROUNDED IN THE TRUTH OF GOD'S WORD, THEY
> TRANSFORM US FROM THE INSIDE OUT.

SWITCH IT

Once you've stopped the lie, the immediate next step is to **Switch It**. Each time you catch yourself dwelling on a negative thought or lie about God, yourself, or money, stop and replace it with truth from the Word of God. Change your perspective so it aligns with how God sees the situation and what He declares to be true.

I encourage you to find fighting scriptures for each specific lie you encounter. A solid Biblical foundation is essential if you are going to stand against the enemy who seeks to destroy you. For example, if you are regularly afraid you won't have enough money to meet your needs, use Philippians 4:19, "And my God will meet all your needs according to the riches of his glory in Christ Jesus."

One of my friends, who served in the military, recently gave me some great advice about being on the offensive in my thought life. He said the military has a pertinent saying for how to think during a gun battle. It goes like this: "If you're in a gunfight, you should be shooting. If you aren't shooting, you are reloading. If you aren't reloading, you are moving. If you aren't moving, you are dead." Wow! The truth is we are in a daily gunfight with the father of lies. He is unrelenting and his goal is to get you to the point where you stop fighting and capitulate to his lies. You must be on the offensive at all times.

Thankfully, we have the greatest offensive weapon available – The Word of God. Hebrews 4:12 says, "For the word of God is alive and active. Sharper than any double-edged sword, it penetrates even to dividing soul and spirit, joints and marrow; it judges the thoughts and attitudes of the heart." Therefore, we have to take up the sword of the Spirit and go on the offensive with God's truth. This means reading the Bible on a regular basis so that we are well armed with the truth, switching each lie that we hear as we go about our day.

> **HE IS OUR INTIMATE AND LOVING FATHER WHO WANTS TO TAKE CARE OF ALL OF OUR NEEDS.**

SPEAK IT

And finally, once you have stopped the lie and replaced it with truth, you'll want to make it a habit. Many psychologists refer to this strategy as self-talk, and there are volumes of scientific evidence to prove its benefit. Whether you simply talk to yourself in your mind or literally verbalize the truth out loud, there is power in intentionally choosing to **Speak It**. It might feel awkward, but it is actually quite freeing to go on the offensive with God's truth. In Proverbs 18:21, we read, "The tongue has the power of life and death, and those who love it will eat its fruit." Paul says, "Let no corrupting talk come out of your mouths, but only such as is good for building up, as fits the occasion, that it may give grace to those who hear."[5] When we speak God's Word instead of believing the enemy's lies, the Bible says that we are speaking life and giving grace to others and ourselves.

STEP BY STEP

Several years ago I went on a trip to climb the Grand Tetons with my wife's family. I am absolutely terrified of heights, so before the trip I asked God for a "fighting verse" to help me overcome my fear. He gave me 2 Timothy 1:7, "I have not given you a spirit of fear, but of power, and of love, and of a sound mind" (NKJV).

About twenty minutes into our hike, as I looked down the side of the mountain, the fear started to creep in. I stopped, closed my eyes and repeated 2 Timothy 1:7 several times to myself. Then I opened my eyes, took a few more steps and realized that the fear didn't immediately disappear, so I just kept on repeating the verse again and again.

Every step up that mountain I was praying and speaking God's truth. While it didn't *feel* true the entire time, I *chose* to trust it was true. In the very act of believing it was true my mind was being renewed. I'm sure our guide thought that I was crazy, but by the end of the day, I had made it the entire way up and back down that mountain without freaking out! Realigning my thoughts with God's truth allowed me to continue the trek by conquering my fear.

As you begin the journey of realigning your financial life, you might feel pretty overwhelmed. Getting your beliefs in alignment is not an easy task, but let me encourage you to keep pressing on – it will come. Even when God's Word doesn't feel true, He will be with you during the process, and you will begin winning the daily battles as you are transformed by the renewing of your mind.

APPLICATION QUESTIONS

Take a minute and push "pause" on your thoughts. What are some of the lies that you regularly battle?

What do you think it would take to begin addressing some of these lies?

Who do you know that can hold you accountable for implementing what you are learning?

When you think about God, yourself, and money, what is the first thing that comes to mind?

CHANGE YOUR MIND

A few years into our marriage, we didn't have a whole lot of money and Jenny felt like it was all her fault. She reasoned that our financial struggles were because she was just bad with money. But, one day, while reading the story of God's response to Adam and Eve, as they hid from Him in the garden, her perspective began to shift. Eating the fruit of the garden and disobeying God had given them a sense of nakedness and shame, so they avoided God. But, instead of condemning them for their sin, God was more concerned with what had caused the fear and avoidance in their relationship. So, He asked them, "Who told you that you were naked?"[1] As soon as she read this, it resounded deep inside Jenny and she immediately thought to herself, "Yeah! And who told me it was my fault that we would always be poor? And who told me that I would always be bad with money?" In that moment she realized Satan had convinced her to believe lies about her identity, and they were keeping her from the person God was calling her to be.

Jenny had followed down this path in her mind because it felt true and it was only reinforced by our current situation. The more she believed the lie, the more it became a self-fulfilling prophecy. In her mind, she was bad with money, so she wouldn't even attempt to manage it properly. And because she believed it was her fault we didn't have enough, she would become defensive whenever I wanted to talk about our finances. The brokenness in her belief system had resulted in faultiness in her actions. She realized that in order to permanently change her actions, she needed more than just a few minor adjustments – what she needed was a complete *belief realignment.*

NOT JUST THINKING GOOD THOUGHTS

In the last chapter, we learned that the first step in the realignment process is to stop a lie in its place. Once we accomplish this, the second step is to immediately fill the void by switching the lie with the truth of God's Word. And finally, we remind ourselves by consistently speaking it out loud or remembering to immerse our thoughts with His truth. As we talk about dealing with lies, I want to make sure you know I am not just talking about being a person who thinks positive or happy thoughts. There are enough people out there who make a ton of money on that subject, but the problem with positive thinking is those thoughts are usually not based on Biblical truth. Instead they are based on selfish desire and wishful thinking. They do not give us what our souls need, a deep and lasting foundation that we can turn to when life gets difficult. You can pep yourself up and say, "No, I really am good with money, I really am a good person," and so on, but if you don't base it on the truth of God's word, there will not be long-lasting power in your beliefs. Simply saying something because you want it does not make it true.

Several years ago I met a real estate investor who had been through some rocky times. During one of our conversations he told me how he had repeatedly been listening to a recording in his car, over and over. It would blather such things as, "You are successful." "You are handsome." "You are smart." Now, this might sound like good motivational reinforcement, but the problem with these phrases is they are merely wishful thinking. He could listen to as many "motivational speeches" as his ears can handle, but it wouldn't change the fact that he was still just a few months away from declaring bankruptcy. Don't get me wrong, it's not necessarily bad to listen to upbeat messages, but when the trials come, they alone are rarely enough to sustain us. On the other hand, when our beliefs are grounded in the truth of God's Word, they transform us from the inside out and will always be there to uplift and encourage us, no matter what the situation.

Changing beliefs is not something that mere reprogramming can accomplish. Simply giving ourselves good thoughts and pep talks might work in the short term, but we need more. Our thinking must be based on something stable and lasting, the unchanging truth of God's Word. The Apostle Paul encourages us in Philippians 4:8 to set our minds on "Whatever is true, whatever is noble, whatever is right, whatever is pure, whatever is lovely, whatever is admirable." As we consider our beliefs, attention cannot be given to just our negative thoughts; we must provide a substitute and switch our focus to the truth of God's Word. This will renew our minds.

YOU WERE NOT CREATED TO
KEEP THE UNIVERSE IN BALANCE.
ONLY GOD CAN DO THAT.

So how does this relate to our finances? Based on what we just read, there are three main relational truths to emphasize and apply. Let's begin by giving focus to the following: 1) Our view of God, 2) Our identity in God through Jesus, and 3) How we manage what is God's. This chapter will cover all three of the relational truths, while the next chapter will dig a little deeper in how we manage what belongs to God.

FOCUS 1 - OUR VIEW OF GOD

All of our relationships are ultimately connected to our view of God. Sin has distorted what we believe about God's character and consequently, has brought confusion into every other relationship. What we believe about God's mercy and grace is intrinsically tied to what we believe about other people, our resources, and ourselves. These key truths shape our attitudes and relationships, and are foundational in determining our financial management. To see these three relationships rightly, we must first start by understanding what we know about God, specifically with finances.

God is Our Good Father

"See what great love the Father has lavished on us, that we should be called children of God! And that is what we are!"
1 John 3:1

Jesus' primary ministry while here on earth was to reconcile the world back to His Father. As He traveled Judea, teaching His disciples and performing miracles, He would often refer to God as "Abba." Translated, this mean "daddy", but in the Jewish tradition, it was heretical to refer to God in this intimate way. It's worth noting, though, that He made a point to call God His daddy, so through His example we would be invited to enjoy the same intimate experience. Jesus begins the Lord's Prayer with, "Our Father," but is actually saying "daddy" and is encouraging His followers (and us) to come to God with childlike innocence in our prayers. Further, we see Jesus use the same word in Matthew 6:31-32, "So do not worry, saying, 'What shall we eat?' or 'What shall we drink?' or 'What shall we wear?' For the pagans run after all these things, and your heavenly Father (Abba – daddy) knows that you need them."

In the same way, Jesus invites us to know God, the Father, as *our* "Abba" in the area of finances. Wow, how amazing is that! We are invited to have such intimacy with the Creator of the Universe, the Maker of heaven and earth and everything in it ... including our money.

If my three-year-old son had the same approach toward me that most of us have towards our heavenly Father, he might get up in the morning and say something like, "Good morning, Father. May I have something nutritious and flavorful to eat this morning? I'll be good." Not likely! He runs to me and says, "Daddy! I'm a hungry boy!" This is the way Jesus invites us to know God the Father as our provider. He wants us to realize that He is not some distant and passive relative that we rarely see, but instead He is our intimate and loving Father who wants to take care of all of our needs.

GOD IS THE CREATOR OF ALL
WE HAVE, SO IN THAT SINCE, WE DON'T PROVIDE
FOR OUR FAMILIES, GOD DOES.

"Which of you, if your son asks for bread, will give him a stone? Or if he asks for a fish, will give him a snake? If you, then, though you are evil, know how to give good gifts to your children, how much more will your Father in heaven give good gifts to those who ask him!"

Matthew 7:9-11

When we talk about God as our Father, we need to put a little adjective in there to say God is our *good father* and everything He does for us is good. One of my favorite expressions to explain the goodness of God is "top button buttoned." If you've not heard this, let me explain. Whenever you start out buttoning up a shirt, many people will start in the middle. But what sometimes happens is when you get to the bottom everything's off. But if you start with the top button, and you've lined it up with the top buttonhole, everything else flows down from there. So, in our lives that "top button buttoned" is to know and understand that God is good. When we get that settled in our heart, everything else is straight and will properly align from there.

In order to filter through our beliefs about the goodness of God, we simply need to ask ourselves, "Would a good father do that?" If we believe that God is sitting around, waiting to discipline us for a late bill payment, then we are mistaken. If we believe He will take all of our things away when we spend foolishly on one thing, then we don't believe He is merciful. Compare this to the picture to a good father. Would a good father be hovering over his son waiting for the smallest misstep? Absolutely not!

"It is for discipline that you have to endure. God is treating you as sons. For what son is there whom his father does not discipline? If you are left without discipline, in which all have participated, then you are illegitimate children and not sons ... but he disciplines us for our good that we may share his holiness."

Hebrews 12:7-10 (ESV)

At the same time, we must realize that a good father *does* discipline his children. There are times when we hope and believe God wants to give us an easy answer or a painless way out of a predicament, but that isn't always what a good father will do. A good father will sometimes apply discipline for the child's own good. We may say to our own children, for example, "This hurts me more than it does you." And as parents, we know there's truth in that statement. We must trust that we have a good father who doesn't seek to harm us, and is always looking out for our best interest.

God is Provider

"Then God said, 'I give you every seed-bearing plant on the face of the whole earth and every tree that has fruit with seed in it. They will be yours for food.'"

Genesis 1:29

From the beginning of creation, God has demonstrated His desire to provide everything we need. In the Garden of Eden, we see perfect harmony, a life where God creates and provides, while Adam and Eve enjoy and manage it. This is God's intention.

"And my God will meet all your needs according to the riches of his glory in Christ Jesus."

Philippians 4:19

When you are tempted to believe you will never be able to provide for your family, take comfort because it is not your job to create provision anyway. It is God's! Your job is simply to work hard at finding the provision God has given you. That's a big deal! We might not be great providers, but you can be great at finding the provision of God.

> "Look at the birds of the air; they do not sow or reap or
> store away in barns, and yet your heavenly Father feeds
> them. Are you not much more valuable than they?"
> Matthew 6:26

Have you ever watched a bird? Does food just randomly appear in a bird's nest for its young? No, what does that bird have to do? It spends its day flittering about, from tree to tree, digging in the dirt, pecking here and there, all to find provisions.

The same is true for us. God is the creator of all we have, so in that since, we don't provide for our families, God does. Like the birds, we simply find what God has provided for us. Many times, due to fear and insecurity, we question this truth. We stand in between the tension of the promise in Philippians 4:19, which says that God will provide for all our needs and the reality of our day-to-day living.

YOU CAN REST EASY AT NIGHT KNOWING THAT YOUR DAD HAS ALL OF THE RESOURCES IN THE WORLD TO TAKE CARE OF YOU, AND HE LOVES YOU.

Early on in our marriage, Jenny and I were in a very similar situation. It seemed like month in, month out, we were barely squeaking by. I met with one of my mentors, asking for some wisdom. He told me to read the following verse:

"'For I know the plans I have for you,' declares the Lord, 'plans to prosper you and not to harm you, plans to give you hope and a future.'"
Jeremiah 29:11

He said, "Josh, this is a promise from God. But here is the cool thing: God created time. You are confined by time and space, so you can't see the future, but God is standing outside of time and can see the past, present, and future. And He sees your future, and He is telling you that He knows what it looks like and it is good!"

My job then is to simply work hard, do what God asks me to do and trust Him. I don't have to know the timing, and I don't need to second-guess that God will provide. My job is simply to obey God in the process and fulfill my end of the bargain.

God is King of the Universe
"In the beginning God created the heavens and the earth."
Genesis 1:1

The beginning of creation is always a great place to start if we want to understand where we stand in the grand scheme of things. Genesis 1:1 says, "In the beginning *God* created ..." Does it say, "In the beginning Josh?" Or, "In the beginning Jenny?" Of course not! So if there's any doubt exactly who is at the center of the Universe, let me assure you, it's not me. And it's not you! It is God who was here before there was a Universe, and He is the center of all things.

When I was a sophomore in college, I lived in a house with three other guys of like mind. Our intention was to get through college while supporting each other in our walks with God. Between studying and an active social life, I had a lot going on. I came home from class one day, unusually stressed; exams were the next week, and the girl I thought was the "one" let me know in no uncertain terms that she did not feel the same about me. Life was hard! The guy who was discipling me noticed my condition, so he sat me down and allowed me to whine and complain for a good ten minutes. After my sob story was finished, I looked up hoping to hear some reassurance that everything was going to be okay. I imagined him saying something encouraging like, "Man, I am so sorry. You are going to be all right. God works all things together for good …" But that's not what he said.

He said, "Hey Josh, I think I know what the problem is. I'm pretty sure you think you are the center of the Universe. And whenever you put yourself at the center, it is always going to feel like your world is spinning out of control. You were not created to keep the Universe in balance. Only God can do that."

"For in him all things were created: things in heaven and on earth, visible and invisible, whether thrones or powers or rulers or authorities; all things have been created through him and for him."
Colossians 1:16

This life, which includes our finances, is ultimately not about us. It is about God and His work of redemption on earth. He was at the beginning, even before time began, and all of eternity will be about Him. When He is the bedrock of our lives, time, and energy, then our resources will be in line with His purposes.

"The earth is the Lord's and everything in it, the world,
and all who live in it; …"
Psalm 24:1

"The silver is mine and the gold is mine, declares
the Lord almighty."
Haggai 2:8

If God is King of the Universe, then He commands it because He owns everything. So all of our money, resources, stocks, bonds, cars, boats, and clothing are God's. It's all His!

When we understand the first two points regarding our view of God, He is our good father and He is our provider, then it's not so difficult to accept that God is King of the Universe and He owns everything. We can trust that He is not stingy and holding out on us, but wants to give us everything we need and actually has the resources to do so!

FOCUS 2 - OUR IDENTITY IN GOD THROUGH JESUS

Only when we have a clear understanding of who God is, will we be able to see ourselves correctly. Satan tempted Eve with the lie that God was holding out on her. He first attacked her belief and trust, and from that point forward her identity in God was shaken. Now, she and Adam were ashamed and naked. We must always start with who God is, and once that is clear, we can ask, "Who Am I?"

We are Created in the Image of God

"Then God said, 'Let us make mankind in our image, in our likeness, so that they may rule over the fish in the sea and

the birds in the sky, over the livestock and all the wild an-
imals, and over all creatures that move along the ground.'
So God created mankind in his own image, in the image of
God he created them; male and female he created them."
Genesis 1:26-27

The Bible gives a clear picture of who we are. From the beginning of creation God gave us an identity and a purpose. We are
created in His image and we are given very specific tasks to manage and accomplish.

One important distinction this verse makes, since we are
created in the image of God, is that we are clearly NOT God. Of
course we're stating the obvious, but in reality it's sometimes hard
for us to swallow. The world does not revolve around us and we
don't hold ultimate power over things and other people. That is a
power only God can have.

"For you created my inmost being; you knit me together in my
mother's womb. I praise you because I am fearfully and wonderfully made; … How precious to me are your thoughts, God! How
vast is the sum of them! Were I to count them, they would
outnumber the grains of sand – when
I awake, I am still with you."
Psalm 139:13-14, 17-18

Another clear distinction is that God created us and has given
us importance. As His creation we are valuable and precious in His
sight. We are not automatons, mere robots created to do His work
for Him. He took time and care in creating you and me, and He
thinks about us all of the time. If you ever have the feeling you are
alone and you don't have anyone who cares about you, just medi-
tate on the fact that God has more thoughts about you than grains

of sand on the seashore! God says that you are incredibly valuable to Him and He is thinking about you all the time, even since before you were born.

We Are Children of God

"So in Christ Jesus you are all children of
God through faith ..."
Galatians 3:26

"See what great love the Father has lavished on us, that we should be called children of God! And that is what we are!"
1 John 3:1

Now I know that in Christian circles we toss around the "idea" that we are children of God. However, if we really thought about it, and if we really let it sink in, wouldn't it change everything? Wouldn't this truth radically change our actions? When we wake up in the morning and rolled out of bed, we'd have a smile on our faces because we would know, without a shadow of doubt, that our Dad owns the Universe! The Bible says He owns the cattle on a thousand hills, and He owns the hills too! Therefore, we don't have a care in the world because our Daddy is the biggest cattle rancher in the world! You can rest easy at night knowing that your Dad has all of the resources in the world to take care of you, and He loves you.

"For those who are led by the Spirit of God are the children
of God. The Spirit you received does not make you slaves, so
that you live in fear again; rather, the Spirit you received brought
about your adoption to sonship. And by him we cry, 'Abba,
Father.' The Spirit himself testifies with our spirit
that we are God's children."
Romans 8:14-16

After the fall our identity was broken and we became slaves to sin. As slaves, we have no inheritance, no hope, and no value. But when Jesus comes onto the scene and we give Him our lives, we are adopted as children of God. The Greek word for adoption is "sonship", which literally means one who has gone through the entire legal process to ensure he or she is an heir. So, as a child of God, you have full authority to everything that is His. That's a game changer.

My mom was married at a very young age and had three kids before she was twenty-one years old. Her husband, at the time, didn't treat her very well and after a few years the marriage ended in divorce. Several years later, she met the man of her dreams and they decided to get married. After a couple of years, they were able to have one more baby – me! But here's the cool part in the story: my dad didn't treat my siblings any different than me. In fact, he went through all the paperwork to change their names and adopt them as his own.

All too often, we commit our lives to Jesus, but we still believe we are slaves to sin. We continue to think and act like we are hated by God and have to prove we are worthy of His love. But if Romans 8 is true, then we are now sons and daughters of the King of the Universe and He is our proud Father! Just like my siblings have been adopted by my father and their identity is now as his children, we have been adopted by God and given a new name and a new identity! We are His, children of God!

FOCUS 3 – HOW WE MANAGE WHAT IS GOD'S

"Yours, LORD, is the greatness and the power
and the glory and the majesty and the splen-
dor, for everything in heaven and earth is yours.
Yours, LORD, is the kingdom;
you are exalted as head over all. Wealth and honor

come from you; you are the ruler of all things.
In your hands are strength and power
to exalt and give strength to all."
1 Chronicles 29:11-12

Another important truth regarding our identity is that we are managers of God's possessions. If God owns everything and we don't, we are either a thief or we have been given permission to use it.

"So God created mankind in his own image, in the image of God he created them; male and female he created them. God blessed them and said to them, 'Be fruitful and increase in number; fill the earth and subdue it. Rule over the fish in the sea and the birds in the sky and over every living crea-ture that moves on the ground.' Then God said, 'I give you ev-ery seed-bearing plant on the face of the whole earth and every tree that has fruit with seed in it. They will be yours for food.'"
Genesis 1:27-29

In the book of Genesis, God asked Adam and Eve to active-ly participate and manage all that He created for them. At its core, this idea of managing our resources in partnership with God is known as stewardship. We don't usually talk about the principle of "stewardship," mostly because we are no longer liv-ing in the 16th century. But the word steward implies a beautiful and powerful meaning, one that we can't really describe with our modern language.

A steward is a high-ranking official who is entrusted by the king to watch over the grounds of the castle. The steward did not own the castle, but there was an agreement between himself and the king to take care of the king's property. What typically happened is the king would travel throughout his kingdom to check up on his property. And if the steward had faithfully cared for the king's property, then he would be rewarded. If he had not, he would receive nothing.

An owner has the freedom to do whatever he feels like with his resources. However, as a manager or steward, our responsibility is to tune into the desires of God and ask Him what He would like for us to do with *His* money. As managers we have a lot of responsibility, but we also have a lot of authority. And even more than just our bank accounts, we are called to manage all resources we have been given, including cars, houses, boats, computers and anything else you can think of. We must continually ask ourselves if we are stewarding all of God's resources the way that He would want.

> "We are God's handiwork, created in Christ Jesus to do good
> works, which God prepared in advance for us to do."
> Ephesians 2:10

He has lined incredible things up for us, His managers, to do good works with these resources. This does not mean we can't spend money; however, we must ask if we are using it in the most strategic way possible. God wants to partner with us, His "coworkers," in order to accomplish His redemptive plans here on the earth.

> "Now it is required that those who have been given a
> trust must prove faithful."
> 1 Corinthians 4:2

The exciting, and a little bit scary, part of being a manager of God's resources is that we are actually going to be held accountable for how we manage. God has given each of us responsibility for His property and notices how we manage those resources. Of course, let's remember, God is not the crazy owner who is looking over your shoulder, just waiting for you to mess up. In fact, in Genesis, God actually gives Adam freedom and authority to name all of the animals as he sees fit. He continues to give us liberty over how we utilize and manage the resources we have been given. However, within the scope of this freedom, we still have the responsibility to manage God's possessions in a way that brings about His purpose here on earth.

"Whoever can be trusted with very little can also be trusted with much, and whoever is dishonest with very little will also be dishonest with much. So if you have not been trustworthy in handling worldly wealth, who will trust you with true riches? And if you have not been trustworthy with someone else's property, who will give you property of your own?"
Luke 16:10-12

One of the things that I still don't understand about God is why He decided to partner with us in the first place. He could do anything He wants to do in this world on His own, but instead, He has chosen to partner with us and place us in position of authority as managers. We should take it as a compliment and an honor that God trusts us!

Manage in Light of Eternity

"But our citizenship is in heaven. And we eagerly await a Savior from there, the Lord Jesus Christ."
Philippians 3:20

Another truth we need to consider is that heaven is our ultimate home. We are called to live with this understanding and approach everything in light of eternity. When we believe that our final stop is planet earth, the way we use our resources will naturally follow that thinking. We will invest in things that are self-satisfying and of a temporal nature. Far too often, I meet people whose financial plans are limited to the "here and now," without consideration for the impact their investments can have building God's Kingdom. But if we believe that this life is only a stepping-stone to our eternal future in heaven, then we will have more intentionality and freedom while we live on this earth.

> "So we make it our goal to please him, whether we are at home in the body or away from it. For we must all appear before the judgment seat of Christ, so that each of us may receive what is due for the things done while in the body, whether good or bad."
> 2 Corinthians 5:9-10

I am not saying that our management of resources is a salvation issue, but the Bible is clear that how we spend our money and the level of faithfulness we exercise with our resources will be rewarded in eternity. To properly view ourselves and our purpose here on earth, we must understand and believe our citizenship is in heaven, and what we do now is more important than we can comprehend. That does not mean we are to be poor or avoid spending money, but it does mean we should be more strategic with how we manage what we have.

To sum it up, before we determine how to properly manage our money, we must first look at ourselves from the inside out, starting with a right understanding of who God is. Believing that God is loving and good, we get a better picture of who we are as children and heirs. We have a loving "Abba," Father, who has adopted us and empowered us with authority over His creation, granting us freedom to manage what is His. What a grand and amazing future our Creator has planned for us! Too often our money problems are a direct result of a faulty and erroneous view of God and His intentions. If we take the time to reconstruct and realign our identity based first upon the good and unwavering character of God, we will be prepared to impact the world with what God has given us.

IF WE BELIEVE THAT THIS LIFE IS ONLY A STEPPING-STONE TO OUR ETERNAL FUTURE IN HEAVEN, THEN WE WILL HAVE MORE INTENTIONALITY AND FREEDOM WHILE WE LIVE ON THIS EARTH

APPLICATION QUESTIONS

How does the thought of calling God "Daddy" change your view of God?

How has your view of God affected how you manage your money?

In what way does the value God places on you alter your attitude?

How does it make you feel to know that God is owner and you are His manager?

MONEY MADE SIMPLE

Now that we have an understanding of who God is and what our identity in Him looks like, let's dig a little deeper and consider how we relate to money. We know who we are as God's adopted children and we know our identity comes from this relationship, but what does that mean with respect to money? In today's culture, money represents freedom, power, and prestige – all things we're taught to seek. Money is the subject of many best-selling and top 40 songs, most extoling its virtue. One classic rock and roll song, "Money," by Barrett Strong and made famous by the Beatles, says, "Money don't get everything, it's true, but what it don't get, I can't use, now give me money." Many other songs paint money as the evil that causes all of our heartbreak, but either way, it is clearly at the center of human drama and wields tremendous cultural influence. With sound bites, songs, books, and blogs, how can we ever really know what's true about money? As with everything, I believe the best place for us to gain a clear plumb line for truth is by looking to scripture for understanding and perspective.

MONEY IS A TOOL TO BE USED

The first and most important thing we need to know is that accumulating money and possessions is not the ultimate goal of our lives. Instead, money is a tool to be used to help us fulfill God's mission here on earth. That is its true purpose!

> "Show me, LORD, my life's end and the number of my days;
> let me know how fleeting my life is.
> You have made my days a mere handbreadth; the span
> of my years is as nothing before you. Everyone is but a
> breath, even those who seem secure. Surely everyone goes
> around like a mere phantom; in vain they rush about, heap-
> ing up wealth without knowing whose it will finally be."
> Psalm 39:4-6

One of my favorite drives is the one from Waco, Texas, to my grandparents' house in Gatesville, Texas. As I drive west out of Waco, down Highway 84, and the noise of the city begins to fade behind me, I suddenly find myself on a vast stretch of road between acres and acres of wide-open pastures. God has created some incredible wonders in this world, but this drive is one of my personal *top wonders of the world*.

If you ever have the opportunity to drive down one of these roads, more than likely, you will notice in one of the fields a massive piece of machinery commonly known as a combine. These mega machines are the lifeblood of farmers and often worth tens of thousands of dollars. Combines are powerful and beautiful, but they serve a very specific purpose – to bring forth a harvest of grain crops, as it cuts, threshes, and cleans grain.

But if someone comes across one of these behemoths without understanding its purpose and power, they will completely miss an opportunity. One person will very likely be harmed, pushing levers and pulling knobs, as he or she tries to grind the machine into action. Another may think its purpose is to look pretty in the field and will "beautify" it, decorating with daisies and paint. Both will miss the potential harvest it can produce.

In the same way, we must understand that money has tremendous power and potential. It is not designed to simply sit in our bank account and "look pretty." It's meant to be utilized in producing a harvest of change and good around the world. That's the opportunity! But, we must also recognize the incredible power that comes with it and unless we apply it for a meaningful purpose and in the right place, it can bring destruction in our lives and of those around us. Money is not intended to be the goal of our lives, but it is a tool to advance God's Kingdom here on earth.

> MONEY IS A TOOL TO BE USED TO HELP
> US FULFILL GOD'S MISSION HERE ON EARTH.
> THAT IS ITS TRUE PURPOSE!

"I GOT IT"

Have you ever had the joy of watching a little league baseball game? It's probably the cutest yet most frustrating thing one could ever imagine. Kids are doing cartwheels, tossing their gloves in the air, waving to mom and dad, and doing anything and everything else but playing the game of baseball. Several years ago my nephew was playing on a team and I somehow got roped into being his coach. One little boy on our team would drop open his jaw every time the ball was hit and wouldn't move an inch even though everyone in the stands would scream, "Get the ball!!!" Somehow, he managed to perfect the art of not moving an inch in the direction of the ball. Then one glorious day, the heavens opened and the angels sang – something in our little buddy's head clicked. It was early in the game and a ball was hit near his position. He sprang toward it, and the crowd went crazy believing that this was finally *the moment*. The world moved in slow motion as he ran after the ball. Finally, he bent over and picked up the ball, held it high in the air and exclaimed, "I got it! I got it!" The runners continued to round the bases as our little buddy stood there in his triumphant, naïve bliss. I wasn't sure whether to laugh, cry, or just tell him good job.

What this little guy didn't understand yet is that the purpose of a baseball is not simply to be "got" but it is to be used to help the team win the game.

All too often, we have the same vision of money, believing that to "get it" is the goal. If we can just "get the ball" then we will be happy and "win the game." Now, I want to win as much as the next guy, but what I have learned is trying to get enough money and things, is not a winnable proposition. That's an endless and tiring game that no one ever wins.

FOR YOUR ENJOYMENT

Please understand, I am not saying that we are supposed to live like monks and never possess or enjoy material things. We see in the beginning of Genesis that God created a tree that was good for food and pleasant to look at. From this we know that God gives us resources to enjoy. But, we must put money and resources in their proper place.

"Command those who are rich in this present world not to be arrogant nor to put their hope in wealth, which is so uncertain, but

to put their hope in God, who richly provides us
with everything for our enjoyment."
1 Timothy 6:17

Paul paints a beautiful picture of how we, as the ones who have been given an abundance of resources, should put our hope in Him and enjoy what He gives us. However, He does caution about our hearts. Paul tells those who are rich not to be prideful, self-centered, or overconfident. In a nice way, Paul is saying, "Yes, you have a lot of money, but it's not about you, Bud!"

He starts by saying, the focus is not on you anyway, and then he goes on to say, "And furthermore, your focus should not be on money either." Even though we have been given an abundance of resources and the majority of our actions and decisions revolve around them, money should not be at the center of our decision-making. Consider again *figure 1* about belief formation, Trust > Beliefs > Actions/Fruits. Paul says do not put your hope/trust in money and, therefore, it should not be the foundation on which we build our lives. Remember – don't put your ladder against the wrong wall.

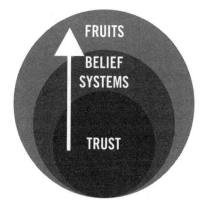

figure 1

Once Paul makes it clear that we are not the center of the Universe and we should not place our hope in money, he goes on to point us in the right direction. If we have been entrusted with His resources, and it's not about us, or the money, then who or what is supposed to be at the center? You guessed it! God is in the center, and because He is a good and loving God, we are free to enjoy everything that He has provided us.

WHERE IS YOUR SATISFACTION?

"Then he said to them, 'Watch out! Be on your guard against all kinds of greed; life does not consist in an abundance of possessions.'"
Luke 12:15

At the same time, we have to be careful not to swing too far in the other direction, with our focus on the nice things God has provided and not on Him. This is called "materialism." The definition of materialism is "a tendency to consider possessions and physical comfort as more important than spiritual values."

There is enjoyment to be had here on earth with our resources, but it doesn't need to be our place of satisfaction. There is a difference between buying things you need (even if they're nice) versus finding fulfillment and satisfaction in what you've purchased.

Some teach the principle of God's desire to provide for our needs, but justify our overconsumption of nice things by saying God is an extravagant giver. This truth becomes perverted when we seek satisfaction, identity and security in those things. We can say all the right words, and even appear spiritual, but deep down we must ask ourselves, "Am I attempting to satisfy myself with my possessions?"

"Keep your lives free from the love of money and be content with what you have, because God has said, 'Never will I leave you; never will I forsake you.'"
Hebrews 13:5

God has promised to provide everything we need, but He has not promised that we will get everything we want, or even that the life of a Christian will be easy and comfortable. Instead, God promises that He will always be with us, and our security and hope should come from Him, regardless of the situation. He never intended His resources to become our goal or sole satisfaction. He has created us to find our satisfaction in Him alone while still being able to fully enjoy the provision He has given us.

> HE HAS CREATED US TO FIND OUR SATISFACTION IN HIM ALONE WHILE STILL BEING ABLE TO FULLY ENJOY THE PROVISION HE HAS GIVEN US.

MONEY IS ALWAYS MOVING

God's intent for money is to be active and constantly moving. We see a picture of this in the Garden of Eden, where God placed Adam and Eve to work the soil. The garden was in constant need of attention – there were times of preparing the soil, sowing, pruning, and reaping. God's natural world is always in flux and continually changing; money is no different and requires the same attentive care to produce a harvest.

"One person gives freely, yet gains even more; another with-
holds unduly, but comes to poverty. A generous person will
prosper; whoever refreshes others will be refreshed."
Proverbs 11:24-25

The same is true in our personal financial lives. God has giv-
en us resources and the responsibility for managing those resources, making sure they don't get out of control, but are used for their
intended purpose. God never expected any one person to get all
the money and hoard it, though some try. Money is meant to keep
moving in and through your hands, and only when it is allowed to
keep flowing does it bring life.

"All the believers were one in heart and mind. No one claimed
that any of their possessions was their own, but they shared everything they had. With great power the apostles continued to
testify to the resurrection of the Lord Jesus. And God's grace was
so powerfully at work in them all that there were no needy per-
sons among them. For from time to time those who owned land
or houses sold them, brought the money from the sales and put it
at the apostles' feet, and it was distributed
to anyone who had need."
Acts 4:32-35

In the book of Acts, we see an incredible picture of how money was intended to "keep flowing." God gives us resources to provide for the needs of our household, as well as the needs of others
around us. The early church had this figured out and there was
power and favor on them because they had God at the center. They
held their resources loosely and freely gave where there was need –
it was so counter-cultural!

GIVING IN OUR NEED

A few years back Jenny and I were able to experience something similar in our small group. One night, we read the verse in Acts 4 about sharing with anyone who had a need, and then we opened up the floor for people to share their financial needs. For several minutes, it was awkwardly silent. Even though we knew each other well, no one wanted to be the first to open up. Finally, one by one we each went around the room and shared. Among the many who expressed needs was a newlywed couple that had recently found out they were pregnant and needed a car and a job. We wrote all of our needs down on a piece of paper, and over the next few months went on a journey to emulate the first century church by answering those needs.

The next gathering, we decided to donate to the newlywed couple first. It was a powerful experience because someone gave them their car, and as a group we were able to give them more than $1,000. The next month another member needed $1,200 for his trip and our group was able to give him $600. Only minutes earlier, his dad had told him that he would match whatever the group gave to him. He had exactly what he needed for his trip!

The next month we decided to help one of our friends who had been faithfully paying off her student loans and was about to get married. Months before she felt like God encouraged her that she would be debt free by her wedding date, but at this point her wedding was only one month away and she still had $1,600 to go. Our group rallied together and that night we were able to give her $600. She was super encouraged, but our group was a little bummed that we were not able to take care of the entire amount. The next morning someone from the group sent an email out and said, "Hey guys, the two couples that weren't at Lifegroup last night had already committed to giving $1,000 before they knew of the need, so the total is actually $1,600!" Our friend had exactly the amount she needed to walk down the aisle debt free, just like God had suggested.

God has created all resources to keep flowing, and when we allow them to do so, we are able to bring a little bit of heaven down here to earth.

> GOD HAS CREATED ALL RESOURCES TO KEEP FLOWING, AND WHEN WE ALLOW THEM TO DO SO, WE ARE ABLE TO BRING A LITTLE BIT OF HEAVEN DOWN HERE TO EARTH.

MONEY IS A MAGNIFIER

"Those who want to get rich fall into temptation and a trap and into many foolish and harmful desires that plunge people into ruin and destruction. For the love of money is a root of all kinds of evil. Some people, eager for money, have wandered from the faith and pierced themselves with many griefs. But you, man of God, flee from all this, and pursue righteousness, godliness, faith, love, endurance and gentleness."
1 Timothy 6:9-11

Finally, we must understand that money is not inherently evil, but it does magnify the condition of our hearts. All too often, people will misquote I Timothy 6:10 and say, "Money is the root of all evil." But, this verse actually says, "For the love of money is the root of all evil." Some people believe that "you can't have a lot of money because it will overtake you and you will become evil." That's not true! Money is neither evil nor immoral. It can only become evil or good when it is in the hands of an evil or good person. Simply put, the love of money and placing more value in acquiring it over love of God and pursuing His purposes is the issue. You must chose – you can either do a lot of good with money or a lot of bad with money. It's what is in your heart.

> "A good man brings good things out of the good stored up in his heart, and an evil man brings evil things out of the evil stored up in his heart."
> Luke 6:45

So, there it is – money reflects and magnifies what is already inside of our hearts. If we have been entrusted with much wealth and we are evil in nature, then it is only going to magnify what is already inside our hearts. When we don't have a lot of money, it becomes easy to point out the flaws of those with abundance because we don't have that enormous magnifier on our hearts! The more money we have, the bigger the magnifying glass on our heart. It is therefore critical to pay special attention to our attitudes about and actions with money. Our goal should be to ensure that our hearts are pure.

We must continue to have our minds renewed by the power of God's Word, asking Him to show us how we're relating to money. And even though we may believe these fundamental truths, there are problematic attitudes that continue to plague many of us. These mindsets distract us and allow our beliefs to be knocked off-track by Satan's subtle mix of truth and lies.

SCARCITY MENTALITY

The first mindset that gets people off-track is what I call "Scarcity Mentality." I have met people from all walks of life and every socio-economic class who are driven by this principle. At its core, it's a negative and defeatist attitude that believes there isn't enough money now and there never will be. This causes us to adopt the Eeyore syndrome – the downcast donkey in *Winnie the Pooh*: "God never wants me to have anything. I'll never have enough. No matter how hard I work, we're always going to come up just a little bit short."

This mentality is often wrapped in a candy coating of Christian asceticism, where we tend to believe that it is more pious and spiritual to say "no" to our selves and to earthly possessions. Now, while there may be some truth in that, the underlying issue is a faulty view of God, ourselves, and the role of money. It also implies that God is stingy and an unkind Father, who doesn't like to give His children good gifts. It tells us that we are not worthy of receiving good things from God. And it tells us that money and possessions are inherently evil and any enjoyment of worldly possessions should be avoided. This can then lead us to a bitter or judgmental attitude towards those who do have material wealth. The end result will be that we feel completely disconnected from God's purposes and avoid engaging in any activity that might produce more money.

What is ironic about this mentality is that even though it paints money and possessions in a negative light, as something that is unattainable or untouchable (and too good for us), it still places them in the center of our focus and energy. We can try to convince ourselves that we don't care about money, but in reality we are thinking about it all day long, just from a different angle. It's like someone who is convinced that food is their downfall so they need to go on a strict diet to lose weight, but then they spend all their time focusing on their weight! Even if they shed some pounds they are still constantly seeing themselves as overweight, and in a negative light.

AFFLUENCE MENTALITY

The second mindset is the "Affluence Mentality." Matthew 6:24 says, "You cannot serve both God and money." The word used for money in this version, is variously translated in others as mammon, riches, and wealth, but it implies much more. The original word is "mammon" and is better translated as "to personify wealth or to deify money." At the core of this way of thinking, we make money into a god or idol. That is why Matthew 6:24 makes so much sense. We literally cannot serve two gods because they are opposing kingdoms and we have to choose one or the other.

In this frame of mind we set money up on a throne to be served and exalted as the main focal point of our lives. We are fooled into believing we are doing it to protect ourselves, or just trying to provide for our families. What we are really setting up are idols in our hearts – all the things associated with money – fame, recognition, security, comfort, success, and material wealth. We will do whatever it takes to protect and keep these idols secure. In our hearts we might be saying, "If I have to manipulate, I'm going to do that. If I have to sacrifice the dreams of God to ensure that I have money and comfort, then that is what I am going to do." Money is our god, therefore, it controls what we will or will not do. We probably don't have a little idol sitting in the corner of our houses, but in the deepest parts of our hearts we are aligning our lives to serve that god.

Because this mentality is based on the belief that money and its associations is our god, it will primarily manifest itself as greed. A definition of greed is "the excessive or rapacious desire, especially for wealth or possessions." Rapacious is the constant craving for more and more and more. The seven deadly sins (lust, gluttony, greed, sloth, wrath, envy, pride) are no longer seen as deadly; instead they are celebrated as the way to true life. Richard Foster, author of *Celebration of Discipline*, says it this way, "Covetousness we call ambition. Hoarding we call prudence. Greed we call industry."[1]

Below you will find a comparison of these two mentalities. Take a minute to read through the list and note the issues that are most prevalent in your life.

COMPARISON OF SCARCITY AND AFFLUENCE MENTALITIES

Scarcity Mentality	Affluence Mentality
Hides you	Promotes you
Tells you to surrender	Tells you to strive and toil
Holds you back	Pushes you forward
Calls you worthless	Calls you lord
Self-condemnation	Self-promotion
Victim mentality	Boastful pride of life
Fights to hold others down	Factions between "us and them"
Impulse buying (consumerism)	Materialism
Jealousy	Envy
Hoards junk	Lusts for possessions
Obscurity and invisibility	Affluence and social climbing
Money flees from you	Sensuous living
Complaining and bitterness	Lying and secrecy
Slavery to lack	Slavery to addictions
Trust in self (not God)	Trust in fame (not God)
Never enough	Living in indebtedness
Businesses struggle and fail	Businesses subjugate people

Adapted from Stephen De Silva[2]

KINGDOM MINDSET

As we begin to reflect on our own lives, we will more than like-ly realize that we, on occasion, operate out of one or both of these mentalities. We swing back and forth between believing one lie one day and another the next. In order to disengage from the constant swinging of our emotions and beliefs, we must fix our minds back on the truth of God's character, our identity in Him and the proper purpose and placement of money. We must align our lives with the clarion call of Matthew 6:33, "But seek first his kingdom and his righteousness, and all these things will be given to you as well." Instead of a Scarcity or Affluence Mentality, our goal is to have a "Kingdom Mentality." When we have a Kingdom mentality, money and life are put in their proper place and we are able to live freely and on purpose, whether with much or with little. The goal is not to have little or to enjoy much, but to live with our hands and hearts wide open, praying just as Jesus did, "Your kingdom come, your will be done, on earth as it is in heaven."[3] That must be the central focus of our hearts. Only when we reach this place will money and life find their proper order.

> WHEN WE HAVE A KINGDOM MENTALITY, MONEY AND LIFE ARE PUT IN THEIR PROPER PLACE AND WE ARE ABLE TO LIVE FREELY AND ON PURPOSE, WHETHER WITH MUCH OR WITH LITTLE.

TRUTH BASED ON SCRIPTURE

Everyday we are attacked with a bunch of lies to try and keep us from the destinies and purposes to which God has called us. We can have the greatest financial hopes and dreams, but in order to experience true, lasting change, we must first begin by restoring the fundamental beliefs from which we operate. Thankfully, God is right here with us in this process and He has given us His word as "a lamp for my feet, a light on my path."[4]

Archimedes, the ancient Greek scientist, once declared, "Give me a place to stand on, and I will move the earth."[5] I believe that the Word of God is the greatest place for us to stand in order to move our world. We must stand and fight the lies that we continually hear. The list below is only a fraction of the lies that the *RE-ALIGN* team has collected over the years, but let me encourage you to start with this list and build your own set of fighting scriptures. The first step in restoring your financial story is realigning your mind with the truth of God's Word.

TRUTHS TO FIGHT LIES

Lies/Truths (Scriptures paraphrased)

Our View of God

God doesn't care about me.

God cares about the tiniest sparrow, so how much more does He care for me! Luke 12:24

God is annoyed by my financial need.

My Father in heaven knows that I need all these things, but I am to seek first His kingdom AND all these things will be provided to me. Matthew 6:32-34

God doesn't care what I do with my money.

God wants to partner with me as a faithful manager of His resources in order to accomplish great things during my lifetime. Ephesians 2:10

God is distant; therefore I have to protect myself.

God will provide for all of my needs according to His riches in glory. Philippians 4:19

God is my protector and my strong tower. I can trust Him. Psalm 91:1-2

Our Identity in God Through Jesus

I am bad at managing money.

The very same spirit that raised Jesus Christ from the dead lives inside of me! Romans 8:11

I can do all things, including managing my money, through Christ who strengthens me! Philippians 4:13

I will always be poor.

God declares that He knows the plans He has for me – plans to prosper me and not to harm me, to give me a great hope and future. Jeremiah 29:11

I am not intelligent.

I have the mind of Christ. 1 Corinthians 2:16

I am afraid that something terrible is always around the corner.

God has not given me the spirit of fear, but of power, love and a sound mind. 2 Timothy 1:7

I will never be as successful as _____.

God has chosen me and appointed me to bear fruit exactly where I am. John 15:16

I am always taken advantage of.

God is a strong tower and will protect me. Proverbs 18:10

I am a miserable failure.

I am not condemned because there is no condemnation for those who are in Jesus Christ. Romans 8:1-2

God's mercy is brand new for me every single morning. Lamentations 3:23

How We Manage What Is God's

Money is evil.

I choose not to serve money, but only God. Matthew 6:24

I am a sub-par Christian because I have an overflow of riches.

I do not need to despise wealth for it is God who gives ME the ability to create wealth. Deuteronomy 8:18

More money will bring me happiness.

I will not set my heart on riches, for they will fly away. Psalm 62:10

APPLICATION QUESTIONS

Is it difficult for you to believe that God wants you to enjoy what He's given you ? If so, why?

Which material possessions do you place too much importance on?

Of the two major mentalities (Scarcity and Affluence) discussed, which do you more regularly find yourself operating in?

What are some "fighting verses" for you to use in relation to your view of money?

PART TWO

REALIGN YOUR PLANS

POWER OF THE PATH

"Show me your ways, LORD, teach me your paths."
Psalm 25:4

Have you ever been inspired to do something incredible? I mean really, really audacious and earth-shattering? Like transforming the lives of thousands of kids by teaching them to read? Or, turning a city, known for its filth and disease, into a training hub for medical professionals? I believe that God has planted His aspirations and dreams, just like this, inside each and every one of us. We get stuck sometimes with our own selfish desires, but I believe God often drops a dream into our hearts and, for a moment, we are allowed to see life as it could be by looking through His eyes.

A few years ago, I had one of those experiences. I took a trip to Zambia and imagined what it might be like to see the *entire country* transformed. At that point in time, the country had an unemployment rate of 70 percent, so my thought was to start a business that would provide jobs for thousands of people. My dream started small, with chicken farms in the countryside. Next step was to transform the chicken farms into cattle ranches, and then, add in a taxi shuttle business to Victoria Falls. Now, I'm on my way. These dreams continued to grow so grandiose that eventually, I began to think about dipping my toes into the copper mining world too!

However, once the trip was over, I got on a plane and made my way back to Waco, then "real life" hit. Somewhere between the passion and intensity of my brainstorms and the realities of my day-to-day life – grinding work and paying bills – the ideas began to fade and eventually rode off into the sunset. My intentions were good and heart felt, but I didn't know how to close the gap between the dreams and making them a reality.

Too often the same thing tends to happen with the grand financial goals and lifetime aspirations we all have. In our minds we can see it, smell it, and maybe even taste it, but we continually allow those desires to stall out and gather dust on the shelf because we don't understand what it takes to make things actually happen.

In the next few chapters we are going to discuss what we can do to close the gap between the substance of our dreams and our daily realities. We will start by talking from a macro-level, what it means in terms of our legacies, and then we will provide a method of aligning the day-to-day management of our resources with those plans.

TRAJECTORY OF OUR LIVES

A couple of years ago, I was asked to go with my pastor, Jimmy Seibert, on a weeklong visit to one of our churches in Irkutsk, Russia. The church was interested in our financial class, so I was asked to teach a financial seminar during one of our days there. But for weeks, leading up to the trip, I was dreading the plane flight over. I am what some might call a "sissy" when it comes to my need for sleep, especially on trips like this. A twenty-six hour flight was not on my bucket list.

On one of the last legs of the trip, Jimmy and I were split up, and he was upgraded to business class, while I was ushered to the back section of the plane with the goats and chickens. Jimmy, on the other hand, got a seat next to a well-dressed man who appeared as though he had found some success in life. Not being sure if the man spoke Russian or English, Jimmy started off with a simple, "Hello." He was shocked when the man replied back with an American accent, "Hi there."

Over the next several hours the two dialogued about life and found that they had more in common than one would have thought. Both had come to Russia about twenty years before for the same purpose, furthering the Gospel and missions. Over the next decade, my pastor would make dozens of trips in and out of the country, starting house churches and making disciples along the way. The businessman had realized early on that Russia was a sleeping giant and there was money to be made. So he ventured out with the greatest of intentions to train people in Biblical principles as a way of doing business, doing it all for the glory of God. Somewhere in the journey though, the business was no longer about God, it became about filling a void in his life for security and fame.

After twenty-six hours of traveling, we finally reached our destination, a quaint hotel in the center of town, while our new businessman friend landed on the top floor in the nicest hotel in town. Even though we were beyond exhaustion, Jimmy agreed to meet the businessman that night after dinner. They talked late into the night about decisions our friend had made over the years. They discussed possible plans to get him back on track, but success is hard to let go of, no matter how broken you are.

The next morning after breakfast we set off to a convention center in town where leaders from churches all over the region were coming to meet. Many of these leaders had first given their lives to God decades before, when our teams first came to Russia, and now here they were, leaders of churches themselves.

During one of our breaks, we went out into the hall and noticed another group setting up for what looked like a business training event. We walked over to a large banner at the entrance of the room to see what the conference was all about. To our surprise, there in the center of the banner was a picture of our friend! He was hosting a two-day training seminar, literally one hundred feet away from where we were meeting with our church leadership teams.

I will never forget that moment. I stood there absolutely astounded. The contrasting picture was so clear and so powerful. Two men, about the same age, had come to the same country, at the same time, with the same intentions, but their paths had taken two radically different directions. Amazing! After soaking it all in, I concluded it wasn't the big decisions that decided their different paths, but rather, their daily choices that led them to two very different destinies.

"The path of the righteous is like the morning sun, shining ever brighter till the full light of day. But the way of the wicked is like deep darkness; they do not know what makes them stumble."
Proverbs 4:18-19

Trajectory is a powerful thing. Two objects can start at the same point and be launched with the same force, but with one degree of variation in trajectory their paths can end up miles apart. Epic legacies and giant failures are both built with the stones of small daily decisions.

Several days later as I sat aboard the plane to fly home, I began to journal what the trajectory of my life could look like. I was reminded of a painting in my friend's office that served as a constant reminder for him to stay on track. It began on the left with a straight line, which represented his life until then. About halfway through the canvas two lines darted in different directions forming a horizontal "V". On one path it said, "Lived for God's Kingdom and Finished Well – 'Well Done My Good and Faithful Servant.'" The other path read, "Lived for Self as a Hireling."

> **IT IS NOT THE BIG DECISIONS THAT DECIDE YOUR PATH; INSTEAD IT IS THE DAILY CHOICES THAT LEAD YOU TO YOUR DESTINY.**

I was struck how life is really about the small choices. Our friend in Russia did not intend to be where he was, but the sum of his decisions determined his destiny. I began to think about each area of my life. When it comes to my health, I realized if I continued to eat unhealthy foods and didn't exercise, the ultimate trajectory of those small decisions ends with me, more than likely, having diabetes, high cholesterol, and spending years of my life consuming dozens of pills each day. Then I thought about my relationship with my beautiful wife. If I continue to choose to be selfish in the small decisions and not look out for her needs, we would grow more and more distant at best and, at worst, our marriage would end in divorce. Then I thought about my two sons ... if I continued to give up ground and be passive and distant, my boys would know *about* their dad but not truly *know* me. And their trajectory would be affected by my lack of intentionality and presence in their lives. I continued to go through every area of my life and write out what the end of my life could potentially look like.

"Then, after desire has conceived, it gives birth to sin;
and sin, when it is full-grown, gives birth to death."

James 1:15

The issues in my life do not seem like major sins or weaknesses, but if allowed to grow, will always lead to a place of destruction. Satan is never content to lead you a little way off the path. He wants to take you all the way!

Talk about a good dose of the fear of God.

But then, taking a look at the other path, what could my life look like if I, instead, chose to go in a different direction? I thought about my health. If I decided to control what I eat and regularly exercise, I would not have to battle obesity, or deal with preventable diseases. I thought about my wife. If I chose to love her and serve her, we would have an incredible marriage and continue to grow in intimacy with one another and partner together on great endeavors. And I began to think about my boys. If I was a present and intentional dad, then not only would our relationships be strong, but they would grow up to be men of power, purity and integrity, who are secure in their identity with a depth that spreads truth and life everywhere they go.

The trajectories of our lives matter. Not just for our sake, but also for the sake of our families and for the dreams God has planted inside us.

GOD IS IN THE DETAILS

"But the noble make noble plans, and by noble deeds they stand."

Isaiah 32:8

The small decisions we make today with our money will have resounding effects on our futures. Each time God gives us a promise, He gives us the resource, but we have the responsibility to play our part. We see an example of this in a verse many love to quote from Jeremiah 29:11: "'For I know the plans I have for you,' declares the LORD, 'plans to prosper you and not to harm you, plans to give you hope and a future.'" This verse encourages us to consider the great things God has in store for our future. But we often forget our responsibility and what is required of us. Continuing with Jeremiah 29:12-13, "Then you will call on me and come and pray to me, and I will listen to you. You will seek me and find me when you seek me with all your heart." Yes, God has great plans for us, but He desires that we daily come to Him and pray and seek Him with everything we have and do.

We all have things we'd like to accomplish, but we must take responsibility for what is within our power to do by aligning our daily activities with those goals. It might be easy to come up with a lofty goal, but the hard part – the part that really matters – is doing what it takes to see it accomplished.

When I first started working at our church, I had some grand dreams. I wanted to see everyone in our church become debt free, then everyone in our city, and ultimately everyone around the world. I was a ball of naïve energy. After our first staff meetings, one of our leaders came up to me and said, "Josh, I can tell you are really excited about this. Now, we've all heard, the devil is in the details, but let me encourage you, it should be *God* who is in the details. In order for you to see all this happen, you will have to make sure all the details are taken care of and that God is central to your decision-making. The victory will be in the details."

Backing Into Your Goals

If you would like to do great things in your financial life, ask yourself, "How am I going to do that?" I can guarantee you it won't magically happen because you click your heels three times or wave a wand to make it so. Simply because you think God wants it to happen will not make it happen. You must be very intentional and clear, developing plans for how to bring those goals down to earth and turn them into reality. Here are a few steps to get you moving from hope to reality.

Envision the Goal

The first step is to take several minutes and think and pray about what you would like to accomplish. Take your time and search your heart as you do this. Consider the scope of your lifetime if you are up for it or, if that's too daunting, think about the next ten years. It can be something extravagant, like seeing to it that there are no orphans in your state or starting a company that provides jobs for tens or hundreds of unemployed people. Begin with something as basic (yet life-changing) as getting out of debt. Just don't feel like you have to come up with a "super-spiritual and super-big" goal. It is just as Godly to plan for your kid's college, as it is to build an orphanage. If you are married, I encourage you to sit down with your spouse and share each other's goals, so you can partner together and bring unity in purpose. Once you have an initial idea of what you would like to accomplish or what you believe God has placed inside your heart, the next step is to begin creating a plan.

EACH TIME GOD GIVES US A PROMISE, HE GIVES US THE RESOURCE, BUT WE HAVE THE RESPONSIBILITY TO PLAY OUR PART.

Get Specific

The next step is to get very specific with your goal. If you find yourself coming up with a very broad and generic goal that sounds something like, "I want to help orphans," or "I want to start a bunch of companies," or even, "I want to get out of debt," then stop, take a few minutes and force yourself to become more specific.

If, for example, your goal was a generic, "I want to give," ask an inquiring question like, "What would I like to give?" Would you like to give money, cars, clothes, or blood? There are literally billions of things you could give, but get specific. Just saying you want to give does not help you get any closer to that goal.

Once you know what you want to give then ask yourself specifically how much you would like to give. "A lot" is not a good answer. Give a very specific amount here.

After you know how much you would like to give, ask yourself, "By what date would I like to accomplish this goal?" Would you like to give $100 in the next week? Or, would you like to give it by the time you retire? Setting a hard deadline allows you to break down the goal into small pieces and determine how much you need to save or give on a regular basis.

If you have a goal that is different than giving, ask yourself, "What does it actually look like for me to accomplish my goal? How will I know I have reached it?" Imagine yourself ten years down the road taking a look back at this goal, and now ask yourself if you can check "yes" or "no" to the question, "Have I accomplished this goal?"

Let's say you decide, "I want to be completely debt free, except for my house, by the first day of next year." Now that is a very specific goal! The next step will help us understand if that very specific goal is actually achievable.

Get Real

Now that you have a very clear and specific goal in mind, it's time to shoot holes in it to make sure it is realistic. Press in here and ask yourself tough questions to see if this is really what you want to do and if you will actually be able to accomplish it.

If I say I want to give away a trillion dollars, it might sound like a great plan but it is not very realistic. Or using the example above, do you really think you will be able to be completely debt free by next year? The objective is to find something that will stretch you, but also will not cause you to quit because it's unreachable. Set a goal that is reachable by working hard, but then add a little more and take it to the next level. This forces us to rely on God and trust Him to move on our behalf. I call this taking your goals to the "God-zone."

Set Markers

The next step in this process is to create several markers along the way to keep us on the right path. Sometimes it feels like shooting in the dark, but planning where we will be in six months, a year, or five years, will help us remain disciplined and hope-filled. Thinking long-term instead of day-to-day requires some adjustment. For example, if we want to be debt-free in five years, then we will want to set an amount to be paid off by the end of each year.

SOMETIMES IT FEELS LIKE SHOOTING IN THE DARK, BUT PLANNING WILL HELP US REMAIN DISCIPLINED AND HOPE-FILLED.

Several years ago Jenny and I were training for a half marathon. We would take our long runs on Saturdays, and a few weeks before the race we were scheduled to take our longest run of our training regimen. That weekend we were visiting my grandparents who live in a small, west Texas town, which is surrounded by thousands of acres of farmland. I thought it would be a good idea to run down country back roads and see some great scenery and enjoy some fresh country air, but only a few miles into our run we realized we had made a grave miscalculation. Running in the country, one quickly realizes there is a major difference from the city – there are no markers. When running in the city, we can tell ourselves we are going to "that building" and back. But in the country, "that building" is a field and they go on forever! It was the worst run of our lives, all because we did not have proper perspective from markers along the way.

As you set goals, be sure to set proper markers along the way. These markers should have a short enough timeframe so they allow you to remain focused and energized, but also spread out enough so you have time to actually do the work. I encourage you to revisit your major goal or goals on an annual basis, create sub-goals for the year, and ensure they align with your bigger objectives.

Actions for Change

The final step in the process is to ask yourself, "If this is my goal, what do I need to change in my life today to make sure this happens?" This is really where the rubber meets the road because you actually have to *change* what you are doing. If you want to give away a million dollars in the next ten years, then that probably means you will need to get out of debt and have a career or job where you can actually earn a million dollars.

ADJUST AS NEEDED

By the end of this process, you should have an idea of where you would like to go. With a clear path and action items, you will know what steps to take on a daily and monthly basis in order to accomplish your goal. The key to success in this process is to allow for flexibility as you work the plan. Every year, Jenny and I sit down, review our family goals, and then we spend some time dialoguing and praying about what needs to be adjusted in the coming year. Rarely have we changed our overarching goals, but we fairly consistently adjust our day-to-day activities. If you realize something is not working, feel free to adjust the plan, but don't just give up. Whatever you do, be flexible, make adjustments and alterations, and just keep moving.

JUST KEEP MOVING

One of the toughest parts about reaching any goal is making sure you stick to the plan over the long haul. Sure it might be easy at the beginning, when you have tons of energy and vision, but it is much harder to keep going when you're right smack-dab in the middle of the process.

When those moments come and you don't really feel like continuing or you don't think you can take another step, the most powerful thing you can do is *just keep moving*.

Several weeks ago, I reached a similar spot in my CrossFit training. I was in the middle of my workout and I felt physically, mentally, and emotionally spent. My heart felt like it was about to come out of my chest – I wanted to quit. I was ready to drop to the ground and go to my "happy place," but one of the coaches stepped toward me and said three simple words, "Just keep moving."

I didn't think I could move another inch, but with his encouragement, I just kept moving. I didn't solve the world's problems; I just kept moving. I didn't do another 100 reps; I just kept moving. It didn't look pretty, but I just kept moving.

So when you are tired of sticking to your goals and you'd rather to do something more "fun," just keep moving. The only way you can get there is by continuing to move in the right direction. We never reach a goal by stopping or going in a different direction. It seems common sense, but we do it every single day. We lose sight of our goals too easily because we forget the power of that simple principle. Always remember, you can do it if you "Just Keep Moving" and let God take care of the rest.

THE ONLY WAY YOU CAN GET THERE IS BY CONTINUING TO MOVE IN THE RIGHT DIRECTION.

APPLICATION QUESTIONS

What is a major goal you would like to see accomplished in ten years?

What in your daily habits would need to change in order for you to make sure you accomplish it?

What are some of the dreams of the past you have left unaccomplished? What would it look like for you to begin working towards fulfilling them today?

Consider using the forms available on the *REALIGN* website to develop your goals. Visit Realignclass.com/forms

MANAGING CASH FLOW

In order to accomplish our long-term goals, it is pivotal we learn the habit of realigning our daily spending habits. We must admit that we tend to separate our desired long-term goals from our day-to-day decisions because we lose focus. The pressure and pace, just trying to survive the daily grind, takes our attention away from what matters most. One of the more practical ways to gain alignment in our daily financial behavior is through a cash management plan. Some people might call this a budget, but whenever I hear that word I think of an old, crusty accountant's office and envision myself with "failure" rubber-stamped across my forehead.

Jenny and I call ours the "Cash Flow Plan," or CFP for short. It is a realistic tool and adapts with how life actually works; rarely are things rigid and predictable. Things change day-to-day, and when we try to operate inside of a rigid plan, we become frustrated and give up. Trying to live by a strict budget can feel like catching lightning in a bottle – it doesn't happen. The Cash Flow Plan allows us to have more fluidity to our plan and adjust to life as it happens.

Even though things happen, we still need a plan for the 75 percent of life we know is predictable. Choosing to plan for the *flow* of our cash in the short-term allows us to have more freedom in the long-term.

CONVEYOR BELT

Whenever I think of CFP, I imagine a long conveyer belt with boxes continually coming in and going out. The job of the conveyor belt is to transport boxes from one location to another. If the conveyor belt is not working properly, then those boxes will end up in the wrong place and ultimately won't accomplish their intended purpose.

In the same way, the Cash Flow Plan is simply a tool to help manage the flow of our resources so they reach their intended destinations. Each month we have a defined amount of money that comes in, and our job is to set up a plan for the flow of this money. The CFP helps us to align our daily spending with our long-term goals.

Too often we see the Cash Flow Plan (or budget) as the enemy in this process. The plan feels imprisoning and is always telling us "no." We believe it doesn't allow us to have any fun! However, that's not true; the Cash Flow Plan is a tool to help us, not to restrict us! If we live by a plan, we will end up having more fun in the long-run because we will actually accomplish what we wanted. As stewards of God's resources, we are to manage the flow of everything we have been given so God's purposes are accomplished.

LESSONS FROM LUCY

I was raised on *I Love Lucy*. One of my favorite episodes is where she and Ethel are starting a new job on the conveyor belt in a chocolate factory.[1] The scene opens with Lucy and Ethel standing in white uniforms, with these larger than life chef's hats, waiting for the conveyor belt to start. The shift leader yells out, "Let 'er roll," and the conveyor belt lurches into a nice, slow, and reasonable pace. Lucy and Ethel laugh as they easily wrap each piece of chocolate and place it back on the belt.

But gradually, the speed picks up and utter frenzy breaks out. Lucy and Ethel are no longer able to keep up with the pace, so they scramble to find places to hide the chocolate pieces they're not able to wrap. Lucy says, "Ethel, I think we're fighting a losing game!"[1] The scene is hilarious, but it is also a perfect illustration of what our financial lives feel like if we don't have a plan. Our objective is to avoid this predicament by developing a plan *before* the conveyor belt starts.

A SIMPLE FORMULA

Sometimes, while encouraging someone to create a plan for the flow of their cash, I hear responses like, "I just don't know how to do one." This is understandable. Sometimes we have accountants do it for us or we have a friend, who is great with money, do their best to teach us. But most likely, we end up muttering our way through it or we just don't do it at all. Creating and tracking a budget just doesn't register on the "fun meter" to the normal, everyday man or woman, who just want to know what in the world is going on with their money.

When Jenny and I first got married, I was really excited to talk with her about all *my* plans that *I* had created. I spent a lot of time and energy creating multiple Excel spreadsheets with pie graphs and projections of our future. I sat her down and *told* her, "Here is *our* plan. And this is what *you're* going to be following." That probably wasn't the smartest way to start the conversation, let alone a marriage.

My sweet, Southern belle took one look at all of my complex strategies and Excel charts and replied, "Uh … no. I don't even understand what's going on there. So, you're either going to have to make it simpler, or I'm not going to do it."

With that, I closed my laptop and grabbed a yellow pad and began to write out our first plan. It started by using the following formula: **INCOME – OUTFLOW = ZERO.**

At the top of the page I wrote "Income," and then next to it I put our sad little number. After that, we went through each expected expense for the next month and wrote them down ... all the way to the bottom. By the end of the page we had a few dollars left over, so we added them to a category until we finally ended with a zero. In its simplest form, this is how you do a Cash Flow Plan. Write out your income, then your expenses. Work at it until you get it to zero.

Going back to the conveyor belt picture, each month we will have a certain amount of "boxes" coming in and we want to make sure we have zero "boxes" without a place to go. Otherwise, they will probably end up at McDonald's, Starbucks, Target, or Wal-Mart (or wherever you tend to spend money the most).

PURPOSE FOR EVERY DOLLAR

When we're creating a Cash Flow Plan, we want to make sure each dollar has a designated purpose *before* it's even deposited into our bank account. That way, when we feel the urge to go shopping because it's "PAYDAY!" we will know exactly how much we do or don't have to spend and on what.

Too often we operate our financial lives on hunches and best guesses. I've met many people who have told me, "I look to see if there's money in the bank account, and if there's money, then I'm free to spend it." But, if we haven't given every dollar a purpose, then we might be spending our grocery money, insurance money, or Christmas money – all of which we will need in the near future. Giving ever dollar a purpose allows us to live our financial lives with intentionality and focus.

I encourage you to develop a spending plan each new season of your life and then adjust it every month depending on your specific needs for that month. This can take on several different forms, depending on what works for you. Whether it is an Excel spreadsheet, an online resource like Mint[2] or You Need a Budget,[3] or a simple yellow pad, the key is to make sure it is written down.

STEPS TO CREATING A CASH FLOW PLAN

Write Out Income

First, write out all monthly income at the top of the page. This number should be the gross amount – before income taxes. Be sure to include different annual or miscellaneous income as well. If there's irregular income, write out the average income from these sources received over the past three to six months.

Write Out Expenses

Next, write out all of expense categories. This is a preliminary run through of all expenses and can be refined later. Place the following expenses in order on your Cash Flow Plan:

- Giving
- Savings for emergencies and purchases
- Household expenses: mortgage or rent, utilities, transportation, food, clothing, and necessary insurances
- Debt minimum payments
- Luxury expenses

We place giving and saving at the beginning of the plan because if we don't, they will more than likely not happen. For Christians, I encourage you to give a tithe (ten percent to your local church) as your first expense. We will discuss the tithe in depth in the final chapter.

Household expenses come before debts and luxuries because we want to make sure we are meeting the needs of our household and families before paying the debt company or buying luxuries. Extravagant spending on clothing or fixing up the "new ride" is considered spending on luxuries. If payments are not for debt or a luxury items, they are what I call the "necessities" for life.

After we take care of our household expenses, we want to be sure and follow-through on our promises to pay our debt minimums. This must come before luxuries if we want to be a person true to our word. 1 John 2:5 says, "But whoever keeps his word, in him truly the love of God is perfected. By this we may know that we are in him" (ESV). So, we agree? Pay our debt before we spend frivolously or go out and have a good time.

Find Average Expenses

Once we have all of our categories of expenses written out, we will need to discover what we're actually spending for each of these categories. One way to do this is to gather three months of checking account or credit card statements. Let's take a look at all our dining out, shopping, and groceries expenses. After picking our chins up off the floor because we didn't realize how much we spent, write down those numbers.

One time I was meeting with a couple that wanted to get control of their finances. During our initial meeting, I asked how much they thought they were spending on eating out. They looked at each other then replied, "Oh, probably $100 a month, we really don't eat out too often." At the end of the meeting, I asked them to go home and pull together their actual spending for the previous three months. A few weeks later we met again and they admitted shock when they tallied up their spending on dining out – it was over $400. What we "feel" like we are spending is rarely correct. That's why we need to take some time to get the actual numbers.

Another way to find out how much we regularly spend is to track it, as we go, for 30 days. This will take some discipline, but it will also help us realize how often we spend money on things not budgeted. Tracking spending will also bring to light spending tendencies – good and bad. One young lady in our class noticed she was spending $2 per day on fountain drinks, which might not seem like a lot, but over a month that's $60. She was so accustomed to this that she didn't even realize she was spending. We have a spending log on our website to help get you started.[4]

Set Your Budgeted Amounts

Once we have accumulated average amounts, now we'll go back through our plan and set a budgeted amount for each category. We have included recommended percentages guideline on our website that will compare your actual monthly spending to what others in your situation might spend.[5]

REVIEW QUESTIONS

Now, it's time to review our plans and make sure everything is correct. Let's do this by asking ourselves three clarifying questions:

Did I Leave Anything Out?

Are there consistent expenses that come up that you have not put inside of your budget? Take a look at the next several months and think about other events that are going to be coming up. Do your kids need school supplies? Are any of your friends or family members getting married? Do you want to be saving for anything special? What are some expenses that always seem to "come up" unexpectedly? Usually, these expenses happen fairly regularly, and we just have to be diligent to plan accordingly for them.

Are the Numbers Right?

Whenever I meet with a couple, one of my favorite experiences is when a husband attempts to put together their budget without any idea of how much they spend on groceries. I love the look on the wife's face when she looks at her husband with a mixture of wonder and disgust, exclaiming, "That's not even close to how much we spend on groceries!" If you are married, take some time and get on the same page with one another to figure out what you actually spend and what is realistic for you.

Where Can I Improve?

This is the moment of truth. Just like my friends who were spending $400 on eating out, there are always places you can improve in your spending. Take some time and go line-by-line, asking yourself if you can decrease spending or do something differently. If you only find $50 a month where you can save money, that's $600 per year savings! Who wouldn't love $600 extra dollars?

ADJUST TO ZERO

Depending on your answers to those questions, go back and make adjustments to your plan until you have reached zero. If you have less than zero (a negative number), you must take money from one or your categories – you're spending too much. If you have extra money (a positive number), you can add money to any one of your categories.

STICK TO IT!

The final key ingredient to living on a plan is to *actually live according to the plan!* What we have found through the years is the actual planning part is not that difficult. Anyone can create a plan – just remember Income – Expenses = 0. The most challenging part in all of this is actually sticking to what you have written down and doing it consistently over time!

Jenny and I have been married for several years, we teach this class, and we still have to live on a Cash Flow Plan each month. And fairly consistently we have to commit to a "re-up" for our planning. It is so easy to grow slack, but unless you commit to living on a plan for the long haul, you will not see lasting change in your financial story. Creating and living by a plan is just like eating healthily. Sure you can go on a fad diet and lose weight for a few months, but true-life transformation comes as you stick to it! Sticking to the CFP can be challenging, but we have learned some secrets that you may find helpful.

> CREATING AND LIVING BY A PLAN IS JUST LIKE EATING HEALTHILY. SURE YOU CAN GO ON A FAD DIET AND LOSE WEIGHT FOR A FEW MONTHS, BUT TRUE-LIFE TRANSFORMATION COMES AS YOU STICK TO IT!

LEAVE A BUFFER

An important ingredient is to allow for flexibility. Even though I am encouraging you to finish your CFP with zero at the end, it does not mean you need to be "maxing out" by spending all of your money. Like I said before, life is not rigid; therefore your plans must allow for the unexpected. For Jenny and me, we try each month to have a little bit of money left over for various events that always seem to happen. We still don't allow the money to float out there in "miscellaneous world." For us this means that we create a "normal" budget with some buffer in it. Then each month we have flexibility to cover expenses that don't happen monthly or consistently. Before the month begins we work on our plan, then look out over the coming month and see if we have any of these extra expenses we need to include in our budget. Then we add them to our plan and rework the plan until we have a zero balance. If we have extra money left over, then we take some time and ask God how we should use that money.

"In their hearts humans plan their course, but the
Lord establishes their steps."
Proverbs 16:9

It's also important to leave a buffer in your plan, in order to allow room for God to speak. Each month after Jenny and I create our plan, we stop to pray and ask God if He has anything else He would like to add (or subtract!). God has all of the wisdom in the world, so it is smart to allow Him some room to speak into your plan.

When electric companies install the wires that hang between poles, they leave a certain amount of slack in the line to allow for contraction. This happens during the winter, and the opposite, expansion, happens in the summer. If they didn't leave slack for the wires to contract, when the first freeze happens all of the wires would snap.

The same principle is true for your CFP. You have to leave yourself a buffer. When you don't have a cushion, it takes just one event or one high electric bill before your entire plan is thrown off. Then you will be the person that tells me cash flow planning just doesn't work for you. It does work, but you have to leave flexibility in it.

CASH SYSTEM

Using cash only for categories that are discretionary (as opposed to fixed categories) is an important step to remember. Each month, once you have created your plan, go to the bank and take out cash for the budgeted amount for categories such as groceries and dining out. This is all you have to spend for that month. We have used this method for a few key categories since we first got married. It has been extremely helpful in keeping us committed to only spending what we have available. If Jenny goes to the grocery store and has only $47 left, then, plain and simple, that's all she has available to spend. This forces us to stick to the CFP without "winging it."

When you are just starting out using the cash system, I would encourage you to start with a few key categories like groceries, dining out and personal allowance. Once you have experienced some victory and understand how it works for you, then you can expand to other categories. If you are concerned about carrying around too much cash, then use gift cards with set amounts, which will prevent overdraft charges. The cash system helps you know what your limits are and will help you develop spending habits that fit within your budgeted amounts.

SAVE CONSISTENTLY

"Go to the ant, you sluggard; consider its ways and be wise!
It has no commander, no overseer or ruler, yet it stores its
provisions in summer and gathers its food at harvest."
Proverbs 6:6-8

If you want to have a financial plan that works in the long-run, you must make savings a priority. Even if this means putting just $5 aside each month, saving money on a consistent basis is the one discipline that will help you get out of the rat race and constantly living in a state of emergency. We always want to live in a place where we trust God with our finances, but that does not mean that we shouldn't be diligent and wise in saving for future necessities. There are two major areas for which you need to be saving: Emergencies and Purchases.

Emergencies

Unfortunately, emergencies are a natural part of life. What doesn't have to be normal, though, is reacting to those emergencies by overextending with use of credit cards to pay. If we start with the presumption that God knows everything that is going to happen in our lives and will provide for our needs, then there's no place for fear and anxiety. If we understand this, we'll realize the provision for our emergency has already been given, but our part is to use what he gives us to prepare ahead of time. This is why, if we have not been diligent to save money in the past, we get caught in the moment and end up asking God or Visa to save us.

Starting out you will want to have at least $500 to $1,000 (or your current insurance deductible amount) set aside in an account that is separate from your checking account. Get this amount saved as quickly as possible. Don't worry if you have to spend it – that's what it is there for, but be sure to refill it as soon as possible.

Remember, this money is only to be used for emergencies, and I'm sorry to say, but vacations, home down payments, and designer purses do not fit the protocol. I guarantee, that purse will not seem as urgent when the transmission on your car goes out. However, it doesn't mean it's wrong to save up for a purse, which brings us to our second category of savings.

Purchases

Each year, an incredible event takes place about four weeks into the month of December. That's right, Christmas. Even though this event happens every year, somehow millions of people "forget" to save for it and end up putting thousands of dollars on their credit cards. In addition to Christmas, each year we run into other events that have the potential to sneak up on us and ruin our financial plan. We all have anniversaries, birthdays, back-to-school shopping, and best of all – taxes! And unless you enjoy paying even more money to the IRS, it's probably best to set aside some money each month for that expense.

As you are working on your Cash Flow Plan, take the time and pull out a calendar and note all of the things for which you need to save. Think in the short-term (one to five years) and in the long-term (five or more years). To get an idea of how much you should be saving, simply divide the total savings needed by the number of months until you need it. List each of these items in order of importance, then go back to your Cash Flow Plan and work them into it. For the Lawson household, we are currently saving for the following categories: Christmas, vacation, car repair/replacement, haircuts, birthdays (x4), anniversary, clothing, taxes, medical needs, college savings and house. That's quite a long list of stuff to be saving for and you might think it's overkill, but I have found that every family has about ten or more items they *should* be saving for. Most of the major stresses in our financial lives can be avoided if we would simply put $50 or so away every month. This amount will vary depending on your situation, but the point is to do it faithfully.

We use a website called SmartyPig.com that helps us align our monthly savings with our goals.[6] If we tell SmartyPig we want to save $1,200 for Christmas in 12 months, then it will take $100 out of our checking account automatically each month. It *forces* us to align our financial lives with the things we should be doing. Otherwise, I have found that if it is in my checking account I am more than likely going to spend it, even if it's "earmarked" for something else. In order to stick to your financial plan, you have to be consistently saving for purchases that are outside of your monthly spending plan and find a way to put them inside of your plan.

NEED FOR DISCIPLINE

"No discipline seems pleasant at the time, but painful.
Later on, however, it produces a harvest of righteousness
and peace for those who have been trained by it."
Hebrews 12:11

If you consistently feel out of control with your finances, there is no better tool than creating a Cash Flow Plan. I understand it will take more work and diligence than you might like, but a little bit of pain up front is much better than years of fear, worry, and anxiety. Take the time and write out a plan, save your money, and stick to it over the long haul. You will not be disappointed.

But let me also remind you, this is the point in our financial stories when we struggle with integrating our walk with God into our daily lives. We are naturally inclined to create a plan and ask God to "bless it," but God wants more – He wants to be right in the middle of our planning. Let me encourage you to continue to invite Him into the entire planning process.

APPLICATION QUESTIONS

When you hear the word planning or budgeting, what feelings or emotions does it cause?

Describe what it would feel like to have a plan for your money and make it work for you instead of the other way around.

Which of the secrets to sticking to your plan will be the most helpful as you either begin or continue doing a Cash Flow Plan? Why?

WHEN PERSONALITIES CLASH

I honestly thought we were fine. On the surface everything looked like it was perfectly fine. But my picture of perfection would soon be smashed to pieces.

We were only a few months away from our marriage vows and things were falling apart quickly. I was the money guy. I was the one who was supposed to have it all together, but our problems seemed too complex for me to figure out. As I sat in the car with my soon-to-be bride beside me in tears, I wondered out loud, "What in the world is wrong with us?"

Several months before, Jenny and I attended a pre-marriage seminar. We talked about all the big topics like in-laws, roles in the household, and most importantly, intimacy. During that weekend we also spent some time talking through the important topic of finances in marriage. We both had grown up in Christian homes and neither of us had debt, so we figured we were good. We breezed through the discussion questions and decided we should probably revisit the discussion about intimacy (of course!).

But a couple of months later the money monster began to rear his ugly head. We decided to take an afternoon and go to Target to add some more gifts to our registry. Two minutes in, our magical time turned into a scene from the World Wrestling Federation.

I was upset that Jenny wouldn't let me register for some "manly gifts," and she was appalled I would have the audacity to put something on our registry that did not match the colors of our house. I stormed off and began scanning Nerf footballs, video games, and the ugliest furniture and dishes I could find.

As we came to the front of the store, a Target employee approached us with a big smile and said, "Are you two all done?" His smile quickly turned as Jenny basically threw her scanner at me and replied, "Yep, all done here!"

Minutes later I was in the car trying to figure out what in the world just happened. It seemed to come out of nowhere and now I was wondering if this was even the right woman for me. She had similar fears about me.

What we realized from this glorious experience is that we are RADICALLY different in our dealings with finances. We are different in every single area – how we view money, how we spend money, and even how often we think about money. We have had more heated "discussions" about finances than we care to admit. And we are the "Money People" for heaven's sake! Talking with others, we've learned we are not alone in our challenges. Every couple has struggles dealing with finances and each other's personalities. What we have found is that to be successful with money in our relationship, we must believe that God has intentionally designed each of us to see and manage money in a unique way.

PERSONALITIES AND PLANNING

"For you created my inmost being; you knit me together in my
mother's womb. I praise you because I am fearfully and wonderfully made; your works are wonderful, I know that full well.
My frame was not hidden from you when I was made in the secret place, when I was woven together in the depths of the earth.

Your eyes saw my unformed body; all the days ordained for me were written in your book before one of them came to be."
Psalm 139:13-16

> WE ARE DIFFERENT IN EVERY SINGLE AREA — HOW WE VIEW MONEY, HOW WE SPEND MONEY, AND EVEN HOW OFTEN WE THINK ABOUT MONEY.

Working with people through the years, we have seen many get frustrated and quit trying because they were convinced they just weren't "money people." All too often we believe that since we don't think or act like an accountant, we must be doomed to fail in our finances. Truth is, everyone is uniquely created by God and has been given unique money personalities. If there is one thing Jenny and I have learned in our marriage experience, it is that we have *incredibly* different money personalities, but we have also seen our same personality types in other people. There are three major traits that make up our money personalities and can best discovered by asking the following questions: How do you get where you want to go? How do other people fit in your financial decisions? How do you handle or spend your money? Obviously there is a continuum inside of each of these areas, but for the most part we usually see people connect with one extreme or the other.

THE FLOATER AND THE PLANNER

The first question we ask, "How do we get to where we want to go in life?" typically has two polar opposite responses that define them. I call these two types The Floater and The Planner.

The Floater

Between Jenny and me, Jenny is definitely the floater. She loves to enjoy life and would rather go with the flow than have everything set in stone. She hates the idea of being "tied down" by a plan or structure. To her, life is more of a process than a to-do list. As a floater, Jenny will wait until the last minute to accomplish something she doesn't really want to do. We jokingly say that the victory cry for the floater is "Victory ... tomorrow!" If she could choose between a straight-line with steps one through three plotted out or a squiggly line, she would choose the squiggly line.

Recently, during a discussion in one of our classes, a participant named Dustin was sharing about his financial situation. At one point in the conversation, he finally admitted, "You know what, that means that I just need to be better about planning." As soon as the words came out of his mouth, he let out an enormous "Blahhhh! I can't believe I just said that!" Even saying the word "planning" made him want to wash his mouth out with soap.

Some of us are exactly the same way. Even the thought of having to plan something out gives us ulcers and makes us want to put our head in the sand. And you know what? That is okay. Actually, it's not just okay. It is exactly how God created us, and that's a great thing.

The Planner

On the other hand, I love structure and am happiest when everything fits nicely into a neat little box. I am usually the disciplined one who set goals for our financial life, and I want us to follow through on that plan, no matter what. To me, life is very black and white and it's more about getting tasks finished and figuring out how I can do them better and faster than anyone else. I know, I'm just a little competitive, but I don't like to "wing-it." I want to have everything lined out for our finances, with a step-by-step process to get us there.

PRACTICAL OR EMOTIONAL

The second defining question is, "How do other people fit into your financial decisions?" There are two broad-stroke types here: those who think in a practical way first – it's all about the numbers. The other extreme is those who think emotionally first – where everything has a deeper meaning and connection.

A story that encapsulates the difference between how Jenny and I view this concept is one we affectionately call the "Cake Story." About two or three months into our marriage, Jenny's best friend had a birthday and Jenny wanted to get her something special, so she decided to bake her a cake.

Good enough, but early on we had agreed that any gifts would be paid for out of our "personal allowance." It sounds like a piece of cake, right (pun intended)? But that month Jenny had already spent all of her "personal allowance" on other items during the first two weeks (which was a normal occurrence for her). She didn't think it was that big of a deal anyway, and she would just use some of our budgeted grocery money to pay for it. Made sense to her because all of the ingredients came from the grocery store, right? But that week I needed to go to the grocery store, and I soon found out that all of our grocery money was gone.

The conflict that ensued was epic.

Neither one of us could comprehend the rationale of the other. In my mind, it was considered high treason to take from one category clearly labeled "groceries" and use it for something that was clearly *not* groceries. Jenny on the other hand didn't think it was a big deal. She wanted to give her friend a gift, and we had money available. We both felt, at our core, that we had been betrayed.

Finally after several rounds of beating one another up (not literally) and managing conflict all the wrong ways, we reached the crux of our disagreement. *We both saw money very differently.* Jenny saw it simply as a tool to show her friend how much she loved her. I saw it as something that should be controlled and used to accomplish a goal. When we overspent with our money or didn't stay on budget, in my mind that was "not practical." It didn't matter who felt loved, if we didn't stay on budget, then we had lost.

We realized that night, Jenny only thinks about the numbers when I ask her to. On the other hand, I don't really care about people and their feelings unless Jenny reminds me and God tells me to!

When that major piece was clarified, it helped us understand where we might find some middle ground. I had to force myself to be a little bit less controlling and allow us to "lose" at the budget, so that we could win in our marriage. I had to think hard about what Jenny was really asking for; she usually isn't just asking to spend frivolously. There is always a deeper story behind the numbers. Jenny on the other hand had to force herself to think through the implications of her purchases and how we could, in a practical way, make her desires happen. Both of us decided to purposely move in each other's direction.

THE CAREFREE SPENDER AND THE TIGHTWAD

The final question is, "How do you handle or spend your money?" Again, we have two general patterns here: The Carefree Spender and The Tightwad. For the most part, we would categorize Jenny as the carefree spender, and me, the tightwad.

Carefree Spender

When it comes to spending money, Jenny has life figured out. She knows what she wants and has already planned out what she is going to be spending her money on before she has it. She is not materialistic, but she enjoys buying nicer things. She regularly uses the excuse, "But it's going to last forever!" It's more about the experience and how it makes her feel than about filling some need for satisfaction. When it comes to saving money, she knows it's important, but she is much more prone to spending what she has now and going with the flow in the future. But Jenny is also an incredibly generous person. She loves to give and sees this as more of an investment in people. If she were an investor, she would probably be more risk-tolerant because she loves to be adventurous and "throw caution to the wind."

Tightwad

I am, admittedly, a tightwad. I have no idea what I want to do with my money and usually would just prefer not to spend any of it. (My dad would be proud of me.) A member of my family gave me a sum of money to buy myself a gift, but I didn't know what to do with it. That was last year and here I am, over a year later, and still haven't spent that money. Jenny would have spent the money in world-record time. To me, the idea of spending money seems like a waste. Each year, even though we have saved up for Christmas gifts, I beg Jenny not to spend the money and just save it up for something else! Life for me is not about enjoyment. Dinner is not to be enjoyed – it is to be consumed. I can go on, but if there is one thing that gets me really excited it's the potential for a deal. I don't care what it is, if I can get it for 70 percent off, I'm probably going to buy it.

Even though I am the tightwad and Jenny is the carefree spender, we have noticed I have a tendency to make larger purchases on a whim. Jenny will spend her money a little at a time, but I won't hesitate to make one major purchase costing more than all of her tiny purchases combined.

Several years back, a home improvement store was having a sale on their lawn mowing equipment. We "needed" a lawnmower, so I went over to "browse the selection." After several minutes I was speaking with a manager and negotiating a killer deal. It felt incredible because I had found a deal and I had won! But once I got home, Jenny helped me remember how just a week earlier I told her she couldn't spend $10 on flowers because we didn't "need" them.

GOD IS NOT CRUEL

"Even so the body is not made up of one part but of many
... If the whole body were an eye, where would the sense of
hearing be? If the whole body were an ear, where would the
sense of smell be? But in fact God has placed the parts in the
body, every one of them, just as he wanted them to be."
1 Corinthians 12:14, 17-18

Why do you think God created us this way? Do you think He is sitting up in heaven giggling because He put two people together who are radically different? Or do you think He gets a kick out of creating someone who's extremely artistic but couldn't create a budget if her life depended on it? Did He do that just so we would end up fighting all the time or eventually end up divorced? Of course not, no way! God has created each of us uniquely and His desire is for us to manage our resources in light of how He designed us. And as we do, there will become an even more perfect expression of the majesty and beauty of God's creation in this world.

> GOD HAS CREATED EACH OF US UNIQUELY AND HIS DESIRE IS FOR US TO MANAGE OUR RESOURCES IN LIGHT OF HOW HE DESIGNED US. AND AS WE DO, THERE WILL BECOME AN EVEN MORE PERFECT EXPRESSION OF THE MAJESTY AND BEAUTY OF GOD'S CREATION IN THIS WORLD.

THRIVING IN YOUR MONEY PERSONALITY

In order to thrive in our particular money personality and in our relationships with others, there are a few key things to remember: everyone's perspective has value, balance one another out, and develop a disciplined core.

Everyone Is Valuable

"The eye cannot say to the hand, 'I don't need you!' And the head cannot say to the feet, 'I don't need you!' On the contrary, those parts of the body that seem to be weaker are indispensable, and the parts that we think are less honorable we treat with special honor."
1 Corinthians 12:21-23

Sometimes, for those who are not naturally a "money person" or planner, it can feel like God has just played a cruel trick on them. Problems always seem to be their fault. But God doesn't make mistakes! He didn't create us and then say, "Oh shoot! How are they going to manage all the money I'm going to give them?" God knows how He created you and me and He places incredible value in us. Our gifts and talents, coupled with how we see and manage money, are unique to each of us. And they are each an im-

119

portant and integral piece of God's purposes and plan. If we were all accountants, not only would the world explode from too many numbers, we would definitely not enjoy life. Our world would not function properly with just one type of person. The money person is not always the one who is right regarding money, and it is okay for you to tell them that!

For Jenny this has been one of the most freeing revelations. One day she walked into the kitchen smiling from ear to ear and said to me, "You know what? I'm not always the bad one with money. God created me like this and sometimes you are the bad one with money."

Unsure of how to respond, I laughed and said, "Uh ... Thanks, I think?"

What she realized in that moment was God had created her in His image; therefore, how she functioned with money was a beautiful picture and reflection of God's character. And if we were both honest, we would say Jenny is more Christ-like, most times, in her management of money than I am. She is much more generous, open-handed, and trusting of God than I am.

Balance One Another Out

"Do nothing out of selfish ambition or vain conceit.
Rather, in humility value others above yourselves, not looking to your own interests but each of you to the interests of the others.

In your relationships with one another, have
the same mindset as Christ Jesus."
Philippians 2:3-5

God designs us differently because He knows what is best for us, and sees our needs in the bigger picture. He knows that we are better together because we can balance out one another's strengths and weaknesses.

God understands I need to become a little bit freer in life. He knows I sometimes struggle to enjoy life; therefore He put me with a woman who soaks it all in to the last drop. He also knows Jenny has grand dreams, so He sets her up with a planner to help her see those dreams come to fruition. God is pretty smart. He created you and me, and knows exactly what we need.

The secret, in all this, is to come to a place where we value each other's differences. Jenny gets so annoyed with me because I'm such a tightwad. If she wanted to, she could dwell on it all day, allow it to fester, and cause division in our relationship. Instead, she has grown to value the positive aspects of my personality. Now, she celebrates my "tightwadedness" because she knows this trait will allow us more freedom in the future. It has definitely not been easy, and sometimes it can be extremely frustrating to be with someone who is completely opposite of you. But when we understand God's perspective and His purposes, it allows us to celebrate the beauty of our differences.

> BUT WHEN YOU UNDERSTAND GOD'S PERSPECTIVE AND HIS PURPOSES, IT ALLOWS YOU TO CELEBRATE THE BEAUTY OF YOUR DIFFERENCES.

Develop a Disciplined Core

> "No discipline seems pleasant at the time, but painful.
> Later on, however, it produces a harvest of righteous-
> ness and peace for those who have been trained by it."
>
> Hebrews 12:11

Regardless of our personality and money style, there are core principles we all need to follow. But, inside these principles there is room to operate in our own unique way, without compromising uniqueness. You don't have to operate like the 40-year-old numbers whiz, when you're a 23-year-old artist. You will only get frustrated and depressed by that. But, just because you're an artist, that does not exclude you from the need to be responsible. If you are an artist, then you, more than anyone else, need to become disciplined in your finances! At the same time, if you are an accountant, that does not preclude you from living a life of faith with your hands open and a willingness to loosen up a bit.

SINGLENESS

The value in understanding personality types does not apply just in the context of marriage. It's also just as important for those who are single. We are not called to live in isolation, alone and detached. It is important for everyone to be involved in community and other people's lives. And God has not created us to walk our financial lives alone either. If you are a single, then the need to connect yourself with someone with a different money personality is imperative – someone who will help you be accountable for creating a plan and sticking to it and, perhaps, help you enjoy life with a newfound freedom.

As you begin to work your plan, take some time to think through the people you know. Identify the right person to bring into the picture to help keep you balanced and on target.

NEVER WANTED TO BE THAT GIRL!

Jessie never wanted to be "that girl." Part of it was pride and part of it was embarrassment. She refused to acknowledge it, but she was the girl who didn't have it together. She was quick to point out she had it together in some areas, probably most, but when it came to managing money, her list of issues ran the gamut: over-drafting from a checking account, forgetting to pay bills or credit card statements. How in the world had she gotten there? Her dad is the king of responsible finances, trained as an accountant and the man who had taught her how to save receipts and balance her checkbook. Oh, and she didn't balance her checkbook either.

Early on she realized it took more effort to be financially responsible than she was willing to give. And with each mess-up, she was more embarrassed and more secretive. It wasn't difficult talking to a stranger on the phone to pay a past due bill; they talked to people in her situation all the time. The challenge was facing those who knew her, those who might say, "You know better than that!" Jessie listened to the lies of the enemy and, little by little, she gradually became "that girl," the girl she never wanted to be.

The truth is Jessie *did* know better. But knowing better didn't equal getting it together. One day, she finally decided that being financially irresponsible wasn't going to be an option anymore. It was time to grow up and become the woman God had made her to be – a woman of wisdom, honor and self-control. Even though it wasn't her natural gifting, she began to understand that the way she managed her finances was a reflection of her character. This was a disturbing revelation for her – something needed to change. So, she brought God into the equation. Thirty minutes of her morning devotional were sometimes spent paying bills because she didn't want to do it alone. She also took practical steps and began setting reminders in her calendar to pay credit card statements and other bills. Things really started to change when Jessie would check her bank account to see how much money she had *before* spending it. This all led to making wiser decisions in how she spent what she had been given. But do you know what helped Jessie the most? Admitting to others that her financial life needed some help. As she opened up to others about her financial struggles, she realized that instead of confession multiplying her shame, it actually released her and gave her more freedom.

Learning to manage her money has been a journey and one she is still on to this day. Though under no obligation to do so, God has entrusted many more resources to Jessie as she has grown in faithfulness and maturity. It is a true testament to His character that He makes all things new, and declares that the present is better than the former (Ecclesiastes 7:10). This could not be any more true than in Jessie's life.

A SUCCESSFUL PLAN

The secret to a successful plan that works for the long haul is to create one that takes our personalities into consideration. If we force ourselves, or others, to operate in ways that are incongruent with how we are created, it will only lead to stress, division, and low follow through. However, if we operate our financial lives in light of our strengths and not in spite of our weaknesses, we will have much more peace and purpose in our financial lives.

APPLICATION QUESTIONS

How would you describe your money personality?

What are some of the strengths of your personality in terms of how you deal with money?

What are some areas where growth is needed in how your particular personality deals with money?

THROW FAITH IN THE MIX

As we work our financial plans (both short-term and long-term), the most important ingredient to add in the mix is faith. It is natural, when having everything planned and under control, to rely solely on our strategies. Human nature compels us, just as in the "garden" to push God out of the process, but that was never how we were intended to live. As in everything, God wants us to live fully integrated lives, where we are diligent to be responsible and full of faith as we invite Him into our daily financial decisions. And when we operate our financial lives with faith in Christ at the center, it allows the supernatural to invade our normal circumstances.

FOLLOW THE RECIPE

Several years ago we invited Jenny's sister over for a "family dinner." That night she was going to try her hand at making sweet potato biscuits. As much as Bubba Gump loves shrimp, I love sweet potatoes and any derivative form they come in – sweet potato pancakes, sweet potato fries, baked sweet potato, sweet potato casserole … you get the idea. Needless to say, I was giddy over the idea of sweet potato biscuits with cinnamon and honey butter! The two sisters went to work mixing the batch and getting everything into the oven. Halfway through the allotted cooking time they peeped into the oven and noticed the biscuits were not rising. When the timer finally sounded, they pulled out the pan and noticed the biscuits were not baked all the way through. They reset the timer and put the biscuits back in for another round. Finally, the timer sounded again and we were ready to dig in. But, something still didn't seem right with the biscuits. Even though they spent double time in the oven, they still had not risen. I was famished, so I decided to go ahead and take the first bite. What I experienced did not match my expectations, to say the least! It tasted like I had consumed a big bite of Play-Doh. I managed to force down a couple of biscuits (thanks to the cinnamon and honey butter), before my sister-in-law finally confessed to forgetting a key ingredient – baking powder.

That tiny, seemingly insignificant ingredient changed the entire experience. The same can be said about faith in our finances. It might seem like we don't really need faith and we can just take care of everything by following a simple, ten-step plan. However, faith is the special ingredient that causes our finances to rise to a different level.

JUMPING LIKE A LITTLE GIRL

I am a control freak and fairly pragmatic for the most part, so this is one of the hardest principles I have ever had to learn. Without fail, God has consistently taken me on a journey of stretching to get me beyond my plans (and comfort zone) until I trust Him.

When Jenny and I were first starting in ministry, I had one such experience. As part of our jobs we were responsible for raising our own support. Only a few short months into raising support, I realized we were not getting anywhere. Even though I had worked my tail off and met with dozens of families, the money was just not coming in and we were falling short of our target. As I lay in bed one night, doubt crept in, and I began to ask myself all the "why" and "what if" questions. I wondered why we had decided to go this route and what would have happened if I had just gone into the business world instead. As I tossed and turned in the bed, I continued to get more and more anxious. I could feel myself in the beginning of a panic attack. I believed God had called us to start this ministry, but things just weren't falling into place like I imagined. As a new husband, I felt like such a bum because I could not provide for my wife. But something inside of me clicked, and with tears streaming down my face I said, "God, You told us to do this, and You said you would provide for us, so I am not going to be anxious. I don't know where the money is going to come from, but I am going to trust You." And then my country-boy side came out a little bit as I gritted my teeth and declared, "Dadgummit, I trust you God!"

In that moment, money didn't start pouring down from the heavens, but I was finally able to gain enough peace in my heart to sleep. The next morning I woke up and looked over my list of people to contact about support. I'm sad to say, but for the first time since starting the journey, I actually asked God who *He* would like for me to contact. He gave me one name. It was a friend with whom I only talked to every now and then, but had always looked up to. Once I got to the office, I called him up and told him about our ministry and how we were looking for supporters. He stopped me in the middle of my explanation and said, "Josh, we believe in you and we'd love to support you guys. How about we cover a quarter of your monthly budget?"

I blubbered out a "thank you" in surprise and hung up the phone. For the next ten minutes I jumped around the office like a little girl. God knew where I lived!

I learned that day, when we believe God and do our part in the equation; He is always faithful to meet us. It might not be in the way or the amount we imagined, or even in the timing we hoped for, but God always comes through on His promises. That day I felt God speak to my heart and say, "Josh, this journey will be less about what you can pull off in your own strength and more about what I can do through you as you are fully dependent upon Me." Jenny and I continue to learn that lesson through the years, and we have seen God show up time and time again as we say "yes" to whatever He is asking and trust in His bigness and sovereignty.

WHEN THE NUMBERS DON'T ADD UP

"Trust in the Lord with all your heart and lean not on
your own understanding."
Proverbs 3:5

But what do we do when the numbers just don't add up? "We have been diligent to create a plan, but we just don't have enough money to cover all of our bills." Again, this is a great place to trust God to be your provider.

Several years ago my friend Vincent decided to go back to seminary and wanted to make the journey completely debt-free. At the time, he didn't have any money to pay for school and to boot, he and his wife had five children to support! He worked hard and received grants and scholarships, but through the process there were several times when it looked like he wouldn't be able to move forward in his studies. Multiple times people told him to just take out a loan, but he and his wife were committed to trusting God and not go into debt. During those three years, they saw God work miracles, time and time again.

One semester Vincent was awarded a scholarship, which he had not applied for, and it covered half of his tuition. Another semester, when problems seemed insurmountable, he walked into the financial aid office to ask for a payment extension, or mercy, and found out his entire semester bill had anonymously been paid. Another month when it looked like his family would not have enough money for groceries or bills, someone anonymously placed $500 in their mailbox. Miracles abounded, semester-after-semester, month-after-month.

In recounting the story, Vincent admits the journey of faith was not easy. It is not something the faint of heart can endure. There will be many times when one must choose to trust in a God we cannot see. But throughout his journey of trusting God to continually provide, his relationship with God was taken to a deeper place than ever before. He learned more about God during his seminary years than any book or class could have ever taught him.

Whenever we come to a place in our financial lives where the numbers don't seem to add up and we have done all the work we can, there is an opportunity, a choice, to go in one of two directions. We can choose to give into fear and take the easy way out by going into debt. Or we can choose the narrow way and trust God to provide for us.

> **WE CAN CHOOSE TO GIVE INTO FEAR AND TAKE THE EASY WAY OUT BY GOING INTO DEBT. OR WE CAN CHOOSE THE NARROW WAY AND TRUST GOD TO PROVIDE FOR US.**

TRUSTING GOD WHEN YOU HAVE AN EXCESS

"Command those who are rich in this present world not to be arrogant nor to put their hope in wealth, which is so uncertain, but

to put their hope in God, who richly provides us with
everything for our enjoyment."
1 Timothy 6:17

What if you are on the opposite end of the spectrum and have
an excess amount of money? Perhaps it seems like everything's
under control and you really don't need God's help? Many of our
closest friends and relatives are in this place; they have worked dil-
igently to provide for all their needs, and are not desperate for God
to show up in order to pay their bills. If you are in a similar situation, it does not mean you are wrong or evil. Please understand,
the challenge is always to make sure your heart is still fully God's
and your identity and hope is not found in your bank account.

"But remember the Lord your God, for it is he who gives
you the ability to produce wealth, and so confirms his cov-
enant, which he swore to your ancestors, as it is today."
Deuteronomy 8:18

We also must remain humble in our hearts and not become
prideful and puffed up, believing that we provided all of our own
wealth. God gives us wealth not to simply help prop up our identity or make us feel accomplished, but He gives us an abundance of
resources in order to accomplish *His purposes* in this world.

If we believe we can accomplish those purposes without trusting Him, I would venture to say we probably aren't fully aligning
our lives and resources with God's purposes. There should always
be a place in our financial lives where God is stretching us to a new
level of trust. Otherwise, life simply becomes a to-do list for God
and we disengage from the relationship and partnership He desires.

The story of the rich young ruler found in Mark 10:17-27 paints
a picture of the kind of attitude we should have. The rich young

ruler approaches Jesus, "'Good teacher,' he asked, 'what must I do to inherit eternal life?'" Jesus replies, "You know the commandments. ..." Still not satisfied, the young man explains that he has followed all of the rules of his religion, since he was a boy. He's pleading with Jesus to give him the formula for eternal life, but Jesus flips the script. "'One thing you lack,' he said. 'Go, sell everything you have and give to the poor, and you will have treasure in heaven. Then come, follow me.'" The young man walks away saddened because that is the one thing that he wouldn't give up. Jesus isn't giving a lesson on salvation here, nor is he scolding the young man for having wealth, rather he is addressing the posture of the rich young ruler's heart. His possessions and position had become the thing that he trusted most ... instead of God!

The questions in our hearts must always be one of, "God, is my heart fully open to using my resources for however You wish? Am I okay with giving it all away? Do You have my heart, or does my money?"

One of my mentor's stories encapsulates this principle well. Over a twenty-five year career he had become successful and reached a point in his life where he had great income that provided a very comfortable lifestyle. He was an elder at his church where he would regularly teach Sunday school lessons. By all standards, he was doing things right. But one day he began to pray a dangerous prayer and asked God if He would dream bigger dreams through him and his wife. God took him up on the offer and invited him to leave his career behind and take a job at a church, making a fraction of his current income. The real kicker came as he realized he was only six months away from being able to take full retirement from his company.

He was torn – go the safe route and place all trust in his wealth, or say "yes" to the adventure God had before him and step out in radical faith. After many sleepless nights, he and his wife both felt like if they didn't say "yes" to the opportunity, they would be missing out on experiencing some God-sized dreams. The power of my friend's story is not in the fact that he left the business world and money to go into ministry. The true power is found in his willingness to trust God with his future – no matter the cost.

BALANCING ACT

I am consistently asked the question, "What is the balance between being diligent to save and living by faith and trusting God?" What I have found is people usually just want me to give them a number to save that is "holy" or "legal" in God's eyes without looking like they're hoarding. But that isn't the formula God gives us (or the one I give!). God wants us to live with constant tension between being diligent and faith-filled. It is not simply an either/ or proposition, and each of us must consult with God to find our right balance.

> "The wise man saves for the future, but the foolish man
> spends whatever he gets."
> Proverbs 21:20 (TLB)

God has created us to save, therefore saving is not wrong or bad, but our approach and our motives for saving can be. Our willingness to give God everything is the definition of putting our trust where it belongs. When it comes to saving we encourage people to have two rules:

Don't Save Out of Fear, Worry, or Anxiety

God does not lead us by fear or manipulation; therefore, our financial decisions should not be made out of those places. We save out of a place of responsibility and a desire to be faithful managers of the resources He has given us. Sometimes those savings will be used for our benefit and sometimes those savings will be used for the benefit of others.

> GOD DOES NOT LEAD US BY FEAR OR MANIPULATION; THEREFORE, OUR FINANCIAL DECISIONS SHOULD NOT BE MADE OUT OF THOSE PLACES.

There are No "Sacred Savings Accounts"

There is no bank account we have that God cannot touch and ask us to give away, period. When He asks us to use our money for a specific purpose and we say "no," we need to dig deeper to discover why. If we are fearful about Him asking us to be more generous with our funds than we are willing, then we need to check our hearts and ask ourselves if we really trust God. This may be difficult, but we must be honest with ourselves and with God – He already knows anyway.

WISE COUNSEL

We must also understand that counsel we get from people who don't share our world-view is not going to line-up with God's perspective. I would expect more than ninety percent of our financial decisions will align with widely accepted and general financial practices. But it is the other ten percent where we are called to operate with a different paradigm. This is what makes us men and women of God. Much of the financial wisdom of today is good, solid, and true, but there are pieces of it flavored with envy, selfish ambition, and self-protection. There is wisdom in planning and being diligent to save, but we must also realize the danger in leaving God out and assuming the position as our own provider and protector. The safest place for us to be is in trusting God to provide for us, and obeying whatever He says to do.

Let there be no doubt that sometimes the wisdom of God does not align with the wisdom of this world. Take a look at the miracles Jesus performed and we can clearly see He was operating from an "other world" point of view. While teaching the multitude at Golan, the disciples came to Jesus suggesting it was about time to send everyone home for dinner, He replied, "You feed them." The disciples must have thought, "Okay Jesus, that sounds great, we will just feed about 10,000 people with the money we don't have!" But Jesus asks them to bring whatever they have, and with their small offering he opened the door into this unseen world and begins to provide for all the people.[1]

The beautiful part about trusting God is we don't have to have it all figured out or provide everything. Just like in the story above, all we have to do is offer Him whatever we have. Sometimes that means we have to work our tail off and sometimes we might have to sell something. But the key is to do our part and bring whatever we have to Him, so that He can pull off the miracle.

FAITH AND PLANNING

When it comes to managing our resources, we must realize faith and planning are not mutually exclusive practices. God has created us to both do our planning and trust Him for provision. In the same way, a two-stroke engine is more powerful when the two pistons are working in tandem, our financial lives will have more power when we learn the secret of planning and trusting God.

APPLICATION QUESTIONS

On a scale of 1 to 10, how would you rate yourself on your ability to trust God to provide? If you are married, how would your spouse rate his or herself?

What is one area of your financial story that needs God to show up? Are you full of faith or is it hard for you?

What do you think it would look like for you to still live by faith if all of your needs and wants taken care of?

PART THREE

REALIGN
YOUR
FOCUS

ALWAYS A BIGGER BOAT

Several years ago, I had coffee with a very successful business-man. We talked at length about life, business, and finance, and at one point in the conversation I asked him if he had any advice for me about money. He looked down and swirled the coffee in his cup, then looked up and said, "Josh, I've got more money than I know what to do with. When I first got started in business I really wanted a pontoon boat. I finally saved up enough money and was able to purchase my very first boat with cash. I loved that thing, but after a year or so, I began to notice all these nice bass boats on the lake. So, now I *needed* a bass boat. I traded in my pontoon and got myself a bass boat. However, as big and nice as that bass boat was, it was still missing something. I realized it didn't have a place for me to sleep like my friends' yachts. So of course, I went out and bought myself a nice "beginner's yacht." And, once again, I needed a bigger yacht." He paused for a second and stared off to the side as though he was watching each of those boats pass by in his mind. Then he set his coffee mug on the table, leaned forward, and said, "Now, here I am today, and sadly I am in the process of looking at a yacht that is one foot longer than my friend's because he just bought one that is one foot longer than mine!" Then he pointed his finger at me and said, "Josh, there is always a bigger boat!"

His words still echo in my mind today. I've seen his story played out dozens of times as I've watched people spend their lives trying to get more. But once they obtain their "bigger boat," they are still left unsatisfied and have to move on to the next bigger or better thing. Money and possessions are simply sand slipping through our fingers, a mirage promising fulfillment but leaving us empty time and time again.

Solomon was the wealthiest man to ever live, and here is what he had to say of the incessant struggle to find satisfaction in things, "I said in my heart, 'Come now, I will test you with pleasure; enjoy yourself.' But behold, this was also vanity. ... I made great works. I built houses and planted vineyards for myself. I made myself gardens and parks, and planted in them all kinds of fruit trees. I made myself pools from which to water the forest of growing trees. I bought male and female slaves, and had slaves who were born in my house. I had also great possessions of herds and flocks, more than any who had been before me in Jerusalem. I also gathered for myself silver and gold and the treasure of kings and provinces. ... So, I became great and surpassed all who were before me in Jerusalem. Also my wisdom remained with me. And whatever my eyes desired I did not keep from them. I kept my heart from no pleasure, for my heart found pleasure in all my toil, and this was my reward for all my toil. Then I considered all that my hands had done and the toil I had expended in doing it, and behold, all was vanity and a striving after wind, and there was nothing to be gained under the sun."[1]

At the end of the day, Solomon realized the same thing my business friend had: trying to find ultimate fulfillment in money, possessions, or work is an endless game that will always leave us unsatisfied. Solomon had everything that he could want in this world, but he still struggled with discontentment.

REALIGNING FOCUS

"Death and Destruction are never satisfied, and
neither are human eyes."
Proverbs 27:20

Over the past several chapters we have discussed principles and practices to help us realign our beliefs and plans, and now the final piece that must come into realignment is our focus. It does not matter if we have a renewed mind or airtight plans, if we lose focus we cannot fulfill God's purposes for our finances in the long run. Focus is the glue that holds the entire plan together and gets us to the finish line. Lack of contentment is the focus of our hearts on something that cannot possibly give us long-term satisfaction. It doesn't matter if you have a little or a lot, the wants just keep coming. We focus our lives on success and material possessions, but those things are not intended to satisfy us. We were created to be satisfied by God alone.

WE ARE FULLY SATISFIED
WHEN WE ARE COMPLETELY FILLED UP
WITH HIS PURPOSE.

Contentment can be defined as being "joyfully satisfied" with His provision and where God has placed you. When we are content, our focus is not on our possessions or our position – instead it is on God and His purposes. We are fully satisfied when we are completely filled up with His purposes. It's no different than eating a big meal when we're hungry. By the end of it we are fully satisfied and don't want anything else. If we are filled up with the goodness of God and everything He has given us, we will not desire to be satisfied by other things.

> "You will keep in perfect peace those whose minds
> are steadfast, because they trust in you."
> Isaiah 26:3

There is nothing new under the sun. Discontentment has been around since the beginning of time. God had created everything Adam and Eve needed and it was absolute perfection. Initially, they were walking with God and were completely content. Their focus was fully on God and their minds and hearts were at peace. Singularity of focus brought peace to their lives … at least for a time.

TWO TYPES OF TREES

However, Adam and Eve would soon lose their focus. In the beginning of Genesis, it describes two different types of trees. We see the first type in Genesis 2:8-9, "Now the LORD God had planted a garden in the east, in Eden; and there he put the man he had formed. The LORD God made all kinds of trees grow out of the ground—trees that were pleasing to the eye and good for food."

God gave Adam and Eve everything they needed for food, but He didn't just give them a cardboard tree that was nutritious. He gives them trees that are beautiful and pleasing to the eye.

Now of the second tree we find in Genesis 2:16-17, "You are free to eat from any tree in the garden; but you must not eat from the tree of the knowledge of good and evil, for when you eat from it you will certainly die." A description of this second tree is found in Genesis 3:6-7, "When the woman saw that the fruit of the tree was good for food and pleasing to the eye, and also desirable for gaining wisdom, she took some and ate it. She also gave some to her husband, who was with her, and he ate it." This tree was similar to the others, except it offered *a little bit more* (or at least that is what Eve believed). The second type of tree, in Eve's mind, is more desirable, offering something the others don't have – wisdom.

If we back up a few verses, we see Satan tempting Eve with a seemingly innocent question, "Did God really say, 'You must not eat from any tree in the garden'?"[2] Satan is known as the father of lies, and this was his most brilliant lie of all time. He attacks Eve at the foundational level of trust. He plants this little seed in her mind that, "God's holding out on you."

Satan used one additional quality the tree was *perceived to have* – the allure of wisdom, but it wasn't tangible. Eve believed God was holding out on her and would not provide for her. If we look at the original sin, we find both envy and selfish ambition. At the center, envy is the insatiable desire for more, the longing for someone else's possessions, qualities, etc. James 3:6 says, "For where you have envy and selfish ambition, there you find disorder and every evil practice." Eve had everything she needed, but she also had this desire for more. Selfish ambition is the constant striving of looking out for one's own interests.

ON CONTENTMENT

We see this same pattern played out consistently in our lives. God is our good provider and gives us everything we need, but discontentment opens the door for disorder. To choose contentment, we must first understand the following two lessons gleaned from the Apostle Paul. First, contentment is not something we are born with.

"I am not saying this because I am in need, for I have *learned to be content* whatever the circumstances. I know what it is to be in need, and I know what it is to have plenty. I have *learned the secret* of being content in any and every situation, whether well fed or hungry, whether living in plenty or in want. I can do all this through him who gives me strength."
Philippians 4:11-13

We come out of our mother's womb wanting more, screaming and crying the moment we breath air. I have yet to see a young boy walk up to his dad and say, "Father, thank you for everything you have given me. I am joyfully content." Normally, they're screaming and throwing themselves on the floor and demanding more food, more drink, and more toys. And the truth is, each of us is a little like that spoiled kid, but now it's expressed as wanting this car, that outfit, this house, or that job. Contentment is something we have to learn, over time, as we discipline that little "wanter" inside of us.

CONTENTMENT IS SOMETHING
WE HAVE TO LEARN, OVER TIME, AS WE DISCIPLINE
THAT LITTLE "WANTER" INSIDE OF US.

The second lesson about contentment is that it's not easily found. Paul calls it the "secret of being content" because it is something that you have to seek out and find like a hidden treasure. A secret is not going to be plastered on billboards or announced on the news. It will be whispered and passed from one person to the next and found through intentionally looking for it.

TREASURE MAP

But I will let you in on the "treasure map" to contentment – know God's heart, be thankful, and guard your heart. Yep, that'll get you there. Now let's get our hearts and minds around these three things. Let's change our focus.

Know God's Heart

Ultimately, to believe and fully grasp contentment and satisfaction is to know and trust God's heart for us. For Jenny and me, the contentment journey has been one of the hardest but also one of the sweetest journeys we have been on with the Lord. Just like Paul, we can say we have been through seasons when we have had plenty and seasons when we have been in want, with no idea where the money was going to come from or how we were going to make life work. Some of those seasons have been really difficult, and some have not been as challenging, but in every single case we have had to choose contentment – without exception.

"LORD, you alone are my portion and my cup; you make my lot secure. The boundary lines have fallen for me in pleasant places; surely I have a delightful inheritance."
Psalm 16:5-6

Psalm 16:5-6 has been a key verse for us throughout the journey. God has used this verse countless times to hammer the truth into our hearts. He continues to encourage us and has given us everything we need, including clearly defined boundary lines. These lines are ours and they might not look like someone else's, but we trust in His promise to care for us in every little detail.

God gives each of us different lots in life. To some He gives extravagant lots, and to others, less extravagant in comparison. But, for each of us, no matter our lot, we can trust it is exactly what God has intended for us. When we understand the principle of boundary lines and are not constantly comparing ourselves to other people, we are free and at peace with the provision He has given us.

It was our first Christmas together, and we spent it with Jenny's family in Alabama. Her parents are normally extravagant givers and very generous, but this Christmas they were especially so. After opening all the gifts, her parents said there was one gift left for each of us.

Jenny's brother opened his first. It was an awesome guitar – not just any guitar, but one handpicked by his dad. He had gone to the music store, playing every single guitar until he found just the right one with the most beautiful sound. Jenny's brother was ecstatic and felt completely known and loved by his dad.

Jenny and I were up next. At the time we were six months into our marriage and absolutely broke. We were so "poor" we couldn't even afford the "or"– we were "Po." I went first and tore off the wrapping paper to see a massive, flat screen television. It was the perfect man gift for me. Jenny went next and she received a beautiful piece of furniture for our house. This was a big deal for her because the majority of our furniture was my old bachelor-pad furniture, which had been snagged from fraternity houses and front porches. As a newlywed wife, one of her desires was to fix up our house, making it a home, and this piece of furniture was her first step in that direction.

If Jenny's brother had unwrapped that piece of furniture would he have been that excited? I think not! It was a nice chair, but it would have meant nothing to him. And if Jenny would have received the guitar, she would have been thankful, but she wouldn't know what to do with it.

As we continued to the last gift, Jenny's older sister opened up her box to find a new purse. She tried to act surprised, but we all figured she had picked it out and wrapped it herself. But as she was admiring the purse, she noticed a pair of keys dangling from the side. She looked up with her mouth wide open and tears began to flow while her screams grew in volume, "Did you get me a car? Did you get me a CAR? DID YOU GET ME A CAR?" As she was weeping, one by one, we all became puddles on the floor.

Several years before, she had been in a horrific accident and was hit by a bus while waiting to cross the street. Her face was fractured in more than fifteen places and she had severe bleeding in her brain. We were very close to losing her. At the time of the accident she was working on her master's degree, so she had to put it off for several months. Because she had to spend so much time in recovery back home in Alabama, once she restarted her master's program she was considered an out-of-state student and therefore had to pay the out-of-state rate. This caused her to accumulate more "student loan" debt, in addition to the mountain of medical bills from her accident.

At the time of this Christmas event, she was driving around the same, old car she had driven since high school and it was constantly breaking down. Here she was, single, with a mountain of debt and a car that should already be in the scrap yard. She felt like she was hidden, hopeless, and unknown.

But in a beautiful picture of the kindness and love of God, her parents stepped in and bought her the perfect gift at the perfect time. It was one of those moments we will never forget. In the same way Jenny's parents knew exactly what each of their kids would love, we have a God who knows our deepest needs. Our hearts can rest joyfully satisfied in His goodness and in His perfect provision.

During that very same Christmas, after we finished opening up the gifts, Jenny and I drove to Nashville to spend Christmas with my family. Along the way we recounted how incredible the past few hours had been. At one point in the conversation, I turned to Jenny and asked her, "Does it bother you that your sister got a car and you didn't?" She looked at me as though I had just killed a puppy, and replied, "Absolutely NOT! And I'm actually a little offended you would even ask me that. Why would you even ask me something like that?"

But in that moment she felt like God spoke to her heart, "Jenny, remember this moment and the sickening feeling you have in your stomach. There will come a day when your best friend will begin building their dream home. And if you take your eyes off of Me and what I am doing before you, and focus on that big house and what you don't have, then you will forget all the ways I am extravagantly blessing you and giving to you *right now*. Do not forget this moment. Someone else will get the promotion or new job. If you are busy looking at their lot and their boundary lines, you are going to completely miss all the ways I am pouring out my love and blessings to you. Don't forget this moment." God knows us intimately and His heart towards us is good and full of blessings. Believing this is worth instilling in your own heart.

Be Thankful

> "Give thanks in all circumstances; for this is God's will
> for you in Christ Jesus."
> 1 Thessalonians 5:18

The second habit for contentment is to choose thankfulness. There will be countless times in your life when you do not feel content or thankful, but the commandment here is to "Be Thankful." It is a discipline to choose thankfulness. It is not a feeling. When we are led by our emotions, we will be taken every which way. Therefore you must choose to align with truth instead of the other way around.

Whenever talking with people about money and the stress it causes, I love to ask, "What would make you happier?" The responses I get are usually very similar. Most want to be debt free and in control of their money. But most also want to get a raise, earn more money, find the perfect job, get married and settle down. Easy, right? But, if these things truly made us happy, then the world's wealthiest *should be* the happiest people alive! But they aren't. There has been an overwhelming amount of study that shows what actually makes up our happiness. Only ten percent of our happiness is based upon our personal circumstances, i.e. being debt free, being in control of your money, getting a raise, getting married, or retiring.[3] So, an improvement in personal circumstances will, at best, result in a ten percent change in your current level of happiness. We believe these events will radically change our lives and cause us to be more satisfied, but after you get the raise or new job, you will be right back to your original level of happiness.

Don't think it's true? Well, let me explain. When was the last time you really wanted to buy something? I mean, you were really drooling over this thing. Maybe it was a car, a boat, a piece of furniture, or even a house. You daydreamed about it night and day and you swore you would never ever ask for another thing in your life!

You finally save up enough money and you purchased that dream item you had been aching for. While science has proven that in the moment your make that purchase, you actually experience a sense of euphoria as adrenaline rushes through your body, what happens next? You have a little "high," but you eventually come back down to a "normal" state of happiness (or unhappiness). We expend so much time, energy, and money going from one "buyer's high" to the next, hoping that one of them will eventually last, but they never do. We must find a *deeper place* of satisfaction that supersedes the circumstances of our lives.

Those same studies have shown half of your happiness comes from natural personality, but the remainder comes from daily disciplines.[4] Some of you are a little depressed after that last statement because you realize your glass is "half empty", but everyone should be encouraged because we all have at least some control over what makes us happy. We have the choice to either focus on our circumstances and hope they will change, or we can shift our mindsets, attitudes, and daily habits and choose to be thankful.

Jenny and I were living in a house that seemed to be falling apart. Each day something else went wrong with it and we were ready to move, but we couldn't afford a new house and didn't know where we would go – we just wanted out. One morning while reading the Bible, I asked God what He wanted us to do about the house. I started reading in I Thessalonians, where it says, "Give thanks in all circumstances; for this is God's will for you in Christ Jesus." I sensed God telling me that His will for us was to be thankful.[5]

I thought it made sense and agreed I probably did need to be a little bit more thankful, but God wasn't going to let me off the hook that easy. He wanted me to actually choose to be thankful. He continued to prod me until I finally realized He wanted me to get off my tail and practice being thankful. So, I got up from my chair and told Jenny what I thought we needed to do.

We walked all over that house and began to thank God for all of the things we had been given. We started with the smallest of things like a new doorknob and then our toaster and began laughing about it. But then we moved onto the bigger things like our furniture, and for the next twenty minutes we literally counted every "blessing" God had given us.

About halfway through the house, we became overwhelmed by the goodness of God and by how wretched we were. We realized we were just a couple of spoiled brats who had forgotten all of the incredible things God had given us because we were so focused on all of the things we didn't have. A quote by the Greek philosopher Epicurus communicates perfectly what had happened in our situation: "Do not spoil what you have by desiring what you have not; remember that what you now have was once among the things you only hoped for."[6] By the end of that little experiment, something amazing happened – we were thankful for that little house. All of the problems did not magically disappear, but our focus had shifted. By realigning our focus back upon God's goodness and thanking Him for all the things He had provided for us, it lifted our minds and our hearts so that we could be joyfully satisfied again.

Guard Your Heart

"Above all else, guard your heart, for everything
you do flows from it."

Proverbs 4:23

The third habit for learning the secret of contentment is to guard our hearts against the constant barrage of attacks. In the Song of Solomon, we find a beautiful picture of a woman pushing back against the pressures of society to fulfill her youthful passions as she repeatedly cries out, "Do not arouse or awaken love until it so desires." Our culture entices and screams from every direction, "Just get this thing. ... You need to buy it. ... It will build your credit. ... Don't worry, you can pay later." Or it puffs us up and says, "Yeah, you go on vacation, you deserve it. ... Buy that bigger house and show everyone you have arrived." We have to push back against culture and our own hearts and say, "No, no, no, no, no, no! I'm not going to awaken my heart to love these things or to believe I must have them in my life."

> **WE MUST FIND A DEEPER PLACE OF SATISFACTION THAT SUPERSEDES THE CIRCUMSTANCES OF OUR LIVES.**

All too often, we are not even aware of how much we allow our hearts to be tempted. Take an inventory of how many magazine pictures, Facebook or Twitter posts, or Pinterest boards you are comparing yourself to. How often do you think about someone else's job, house, car, or spouse? We fill our minds with all the things we don't have and it creates a longing inside of our hearts for things outside of our boundary lines. For some of you, it might be healthy to go through and unsubscribe from the dozens of email and magazine subscriptions that cause you to compare yourself to others. Maybe you need to cut off cable television or go "off-line" with all social media. If the heart denotes a person's center for both physical and emotional-intellectual-moral activities, then we must do whatever it takes to guard the purity of everything that flows into it.

SOMETHING BETTER

"Do you not know that in a race all the runners run, but only one gets the prize? Run in such a way as to get the prize. Every-one who competes in the games goes into strict training. They do it to get a crown that will not last, but we do it to get a crown that will last forever. Therefore I do not run like someone run-ning aimlessly; I do not fight like a boxer beating the air. No, I strike a blow to my body and make it my slave so that after I have preached to others, I myself will not be disqualified for the prize."
1 Corinthians 9:24-27

DO NOT SPOIL WHAT YOU HAVE BY DESIRING WHAT YOU HAVE NOT; REMEMBER THAT WHAT YOU NOW HAVE WAS ONCE AMONG THE THINGS YOU ONLY HOPED FOR.

In the 1970's there was a study done by psychologist Walter Mischel testing the ability of young children to delay their desire for instant gratification.[7] He placed a cookie in front of each child and then presented them with two options: go ahead and eat the cookie, or wait until he returned and they would be given a second cookie. Many of the children were unable to resist the temptation to eat the cookie now (which is completely understandable!), however, a handful were able to hold out for the doubled reward. They were termed "high-delay children" and, compared with the others, went on to score higher on standardized test, complete their secondary education at a higher rate, and earn higher incomes. Those findings alone should be a great encouragement for us all to learn delayed gratification and pass it on to our kids!

What can we learn from the kids who were able to say "no" to cookies? The children are not any more disciplined than the other kids nor did they have some supernatural willpower. They had simply practiced a secret we can all use to help us say no – distraction. This is what we need to learn to do with temptations. Discipline ourselves to guard our hearts with a strategy of replacing the temptations with something better – righteousness and peace from God.

"No discipline seems pleasant at the time, but painful. Later on, however, it produces a harvest of righteousness and peace for those who have been trained by it."
Hebrews 12:11

In order to learn the secret of contentment, we must learn how to implement this practice of distracting and refocusing our minds and our hearts onto the better things that God has already provided for us and will provide for us in the future. The writer of Hebrews tapped into this idea. Discipline is never fun, but the harvest it allows us to have later on will be well worth it. We have to distract ourselves with what that "better harvest" will look like, feel like, and taste like for us to have the power to say "no" to the temptations immediately before us.

"Finally, brothers and sisters, whatever is true,
whatever is noble, whatever is right, whatever is pure,
whatever is lovely, whatever is admirable – if anything is
excellent or praiseworthy – think about such things"
Philippians 4:8

The journey of contentment is not an easy one. For us personally, it is a lesson Jenny and I have had to continue to work on again and again. We are the couple that gives the "Contentment Talk" and we daily have to choose to be content and thankful for where God has us and what He has given to us. The key in this journey has been to find our rest and contentment not just in the things we have, but in the fact Jesus is with us. This idea is summed up in the Hebrews 13:5, "Keep your lives free from the love of money and be content with what you have, because God has said, 'Never will I leave you; never will I forsake you.'"

APPLICATION QUESTIONS

In what ways are you discontent?

How does knowing God's heart for you change your level of contentment?

What are some ways you can guard your heart?

DESTRUCTIVE DEBT STORY

We have met with hundreds of families who were drowning in debt, but one family perfectly exemplifies the "Destructive Debt Story." Since beginning our classes, there have been only a few couples with more consumer debt than Charles and his wife – they were very creative and found every possible way to get deeper in debt.

Their debt story began like many others. They fell in love and knew they would spend the rest of their lives together, so Charles decided to head off to the jewelry store to buy a ring. He couldn't afford the ring he wanted, so the jewelry salesman "helped" him out by giving him a payment plan (in addition to throwing in the band and some earrings). This should have been a sign of things to come.

They also both brought into marriage the beautiful gift of student loan debt. The loans were at a great rate so they decided to delay paying off the principal and kept making minimum payments.

Charles took a job, where he traveled extensively, so he "had" to get a new car. His wife liked the look and smell of his new car and decided she "needed" one too. They soon began piling up credit card debt on one card, but it soon maxed out, so they added another one. Then another. And another. Eventually they hit the limit on every card. But thankfully a credit consolidation company "helped" them out and gave them a little breathing room, so within a few months they were able to start using those credit cards again.

In the midst of all of this, Charles lost his job and their lives were turned upside down. They decided to move, but moving is expensive, so the credit cards soon became their only lifeline. His new job didn't pay enough to cover all their expenses and the debt payments, so several weeks in a row they found themselves charging groceries on credit cards, hoping the future would be better. When things became unbearable, the in-laws allowed them to move-in with them and "helped" them out by loaning them even more money.

Finally, Charles landed a great job that could cover all of their debt payments and regular bills with a little left over. With this little extra cash each month, they could have paid down their debt, but instead they decided they "needed" to buy a new house. And what does every new house need? Furniture! Their credit cards were maxed out, but thankfully the furniture company "helped" them out by giving them an easy payment plan.

By the time we met with them, they had accumulated almost $115,000 in debt, not including their house. They were tired and worn out. Along the way they had met many "helpful" people, people who sold them things they wanted with easy payment plans. However, at the end of the day, they realized those people weren't helping at all. They were drowning in debt and their marriage was under constant tension, but they did it to themselves.

WHEREVER YOU ARE IN YOUR FINANCIAL STORY, THERE IS A WAY FOR YOU TO BE DEBT FREE.

NOT UNCOMMON

Sadly, Charles' story is not much different than many of the families we meet, and maybe it's not much different than yours. Perhaps you have become accustomed to thinking debt is just a normal part of life and you will always be stuck with it. You have plenty of nice things, but they are all on payment plans and, more than likely, you're upside down. Or maybe you made some mistakes and you find yourself with a wad of debt looming over your head and you're not sure what to do about it. You might even be the rare exception, with no debt, but you always feel like, at any moment, it could happen to you. Wherever you are in your financial story, I believe there is a way for you to be debt free.

In order to become debt free, we first need to understand what got us there in the first place. There are four major causes for debt that typically get us to this point. These debts are destroying people's financial stories and keeping them from the financial future that God desires.

> IN ORDER TO BECOME DEBT FREE,
> WE FIRST NEED TO UNDERSTAND WHAT GOT US
> THERE IN THE FIRST PLACE.

STUDENT LOANS

Without fail, in every single class we offer, student loans are always the number one and largest source of debt. That surprised me, but it is usually close to half of the entire debt load of our classes. In America, the average debt load for graduating seniors is over

$35,000.[1] It is now the norm for young people to rack up tens of thousands and sometimes even, hundreds of thousands of dollars in student loan debt before the time they are twenty-two years old.

I believe the college tuition system is broken across the board and will eventually have to undergo an entire overhaul much like the mortgage and healthcare systems. However, in the meantime, it is hamstringing millions of our young people every single year. I wholeheartedly believe in getting a great education, but I do not agree with leveraging the next ten or twenty years' worth of your paycheck for a piece of paper. There are ways to avoid this debt and I have explained in detail how you can go through college debt free in my book *Don't Get Suckered: How to Graduate College Debt Free … and with Your Shirt*.

Student loans are often an overwhelming debt, but they are simply a primer for a lifetime of accumulating other types of debt. They are training our young to accept a life of slavery to the debt monster.

CREDIT CARDS

The next major type of debt ruining our financial futures is credit card debt. A recent survey disclosed that close to half of American households are carrying a balance on their credit cards.[2] That means each month hundreds of millions of people are losing money to interest and fees.

Credit card companies make money two basic ways: fees (transaction fees, late fees, over-limit fees, transfer fees, and annual fees) and interest charges on outstanding balances.

When we understand how they make money, it is easy to see why they spend so much on marketing themselves as our "savior" when life events hit us. They know your car is going to break down. They know you might lose your job. They know those cute red shoes are just "to die for." And they have positioned themselves perfectly so they are there for you when you "need it." And then they allow you to pay it off little by little, all because they are your "friend."

Credit Scores

I hear this all the time; "My parents told me I need to get a credit card in order to improve my credit score." This terrifies me because giving a credit card to a college student is like asking a three year old to walk a Great Dane – eventually that kid is going to get their face drug through the dirt. Granted, in our current economic culture, we are driven by the credit score, whether it is for a cell phone or down payment on a house, but we also need to realize the credit score simply shows your ability to pay down debt so you can get more of it.[3] If you still feel the need to get a credit card, I would encourage you to take a full year (that's right – a year) and live on a budget, and then see if you are ready for the enormous responsibility and temptation of having one.

For a very miniscule percentage of the population, credit cards are *okay*. If you are an *extremely* disciplined person and have consistently been living on a financial plan and budget, and most importantly, you can pay off your credit cards each month, then you can consider a credit card. Again, back to the Great Dane imagery – you need to have enough financial muscle and discipline to be able to keep it in your control. It should be said, though, that studies have shown you spend more when you use plastic than when you use cash.[4] Here are a few simple rules for using credit cards with wisdom.

Rules for Wise Credit Card Use

- Only use credit cards for bills or budgeted expenses. Do not use it for discretionary spending like shopping, dining out, groceries, or vacations. And do not use a credit card for emergencies! This is what an emergency fund covers.

- Pay balances in full each month … NO MATTER WHAT! Set a reminder for the bill date and do whatever it takes to make sure the bill gets paid.
- Track spending against your checking account. If you have spent money on the credit card, then you should keep a running total of how much you will have to be paying out of your checking account to pay off the balance at the end of the month. Otherwise, we get caught without enough money in the account to pay it off.
- Set-up an automatic payment so a payment is never missed.
- If you ever get off track or out of control, then you must stop it. It's okay to admit you aren't ready for a credit card. Some people never are. If you find yourself having trouble paying your balance in full or tracking your spending, cut up your card, throw it in the trash and cancel it. I would also tell a close friend about your decision.

Juggling Flaming Chainsaws

I NEVER encourage credit cards for young people, for those who are just getting started and learning how to manage their resources, for those who have a history of being addicted to shopping or overspending, or for those who have racked up credit card debt in the past. I think they would be better off learning how to juggle flaming chainsaws. I'm not going to give a beer to an alcoholic, and I would never give a credit card to someone who has been in debt or financial troubles in the past.

AUTO LOANS

The third major debt I have seen ruin people's financial lives is auto loans. I was talking with a family member about their new car and they said to me, "Oh, Josh, we will always have a car payment!" Just like student loan debt has become the norm for an entire generation, car loans have been the standard in our culture for decades.

Currently, the average new car payment in America is $450 per month.[5] That is just the "average" car payment. Imagine what happens when you have a family with multiple cars! Behind student loan debt, the second highest consumer debt for families is on cars. This is true for the families in our *REALIGN* classes too.

For the most part, people know they shouldn't be paying hundreds of dollars or even thousands of dollars each month for a car, but our culture compels us to think we are weird if we aren't driving around the newest car with all the bells and whistles. Without fail there is always a "yeah ... but" story behind why they have cars they can't really afford. I consistently hear people say, "Yeah, I know this car is draining our finances, but I couldn't drive an older or smaller car because they just aren't safe!" We choose to pay thousands of dollars each year so we can drive military grade armored cars to chauffeur our kids around town! Really?

We should ask ourselves, why we are getting that car instead of driving around a clunker and saving up for a better used one. Is it because we want to look like we're important? Is it because the clunker makes us feel insecure and broke? Is it because we want to show off how much money "we don't have"? Is it car lust? Well, car lust and trying to look cool for the neighbors is keeping us from being financially free!

HOME, SWEET AND SOUR HOME

The fourth major debt is home mortgages. Our homes should be a place of tranquility, peace, and rest, but all too often families come to hate their homes because they are living in a place they cannot afford. One of the most frequently searched phrases online, when it comes to personal finances is, "How much house can I afford?" This is simply the wrong question to be asking. Instead of asking, "How big of a house can we get?" we should be asking ourselves what is the right size home for our family that is realistically affordable.

Obviously, in our current real estate market, it is nearly impossible to pay cash for a house (even though Jenny and I are going to try our hardest!). So when it comes to getting a house, what do we do? Here are a few strategies to keep us from overleveraging our lives on a house:

Buy a Home You Need

Too often "wants" become our needs, especially when it comes to our homes. Simply because we don't want to be uncomfortable or we are comparing ourselves to what others have, we overspend. Fifty years ago the average home was barely more than 1,000 square feet! Consider buying a home that is a reasonable size and price, and then save your money for your kids' college!

Before we even begin thinking about buying a home we need to have two things in order: First, we need to be living on a plan so we know how much we can realistically afford. Secondly, we need to have an emergency fund established because, without fail, we will have something go wrong in the house.

> **TOO OFTEN "WANTS" BECOME OUR NEEDS, ESPECIALLY WHEN IT COMES TO OUR HOMES.**

If you have to get a mortgage, I encourage you to get a 15-year note and work hard to pay it off as quickly as possible. This will force you into a "normal-sized" or "right-sized" home, and will end up saving thousands of dollars in the long run.

WHAT DOES THE BIBLE SAY ABOUT DEBT?

Even though our culture and economic systems are very different than those found in the Bible, we look to the Bible to understand what God says about debt as a principle. Throughout the Old Testament debt was seen as something that should be avoided at all costs. In Deuteronomy 28 debt is actually mentioned as a curse that comes upon the children of Israel due to their disobedience. Proverbs 22:7 says, "The rich rule over the poor and the borrower is slave to the lender." Solomon tells us that when we borrow money, we become a servant of whoever is lending us the money. When you put this verse in direct comparison to the charge found in I Corinthians 7:23, "You were bought at a price; do not become slaves of human beings," we realize debt is not seen as a place of glory or honor in the Bible. Let me be clear, it is nowhere communicated debt is a sin, but it is clear we should avoid it and if we are in debt, we should understand why we're there and do whatever it takes to get out of it.

STEPS TO GET OUT OF DEBT

If you are already in a place where you have accumulated debt, it is time to get serious about becoming debt free. Don't let it loom over your head any longer. Each day you allow your debt to linger, it is another day your future joy and destiny is delayed. Today is the best day you have to get started on the journey to freedom. As you begin the journey towards freedom, here are five steps you must commit to right from the start to get out of debt.

- **Pray** - The most important thing we can do as we begin in this journey is to deepen our relationship with God. He wants us to be debt free more than we do, and He will give us hope and encouragement along the way.
- **Save** - Before we begin paying off our debt, we need to set aside a small savings account in case an emergency happens. That way, if something does come up while we're paying off our debt, we are able to stick to our Cash Flow Plan and not take on any more debt.
- **Commit** - Next, we must commit to getting out of debt no matter what it takes. I promise you there will be times when it's just hard, but the pain of being in debt for the rest of your life greatly outweighs the pain of making the difficult decisions to become debt free today. If you get serious about becoming debt free, I guarantee you there will be sacrifices along the way that won't be easy, but it will be needed and worth it. Too often people want the easy way out or hope for a long lost wealthy uncle to suddenly write them a check. You won't have a rich uncle, I can promise you that. It will take hard work on your part to get out of the place you are. We have found, on average, our class participants are able to become debt free in two to five years.
- **Ally** - We all need to have someone walking with us through this process. It will be challenging and there will be discouragements along the way, so having the support of an encouraging friend will help us stay the course. Obviously, if you are married, you will want to be in agreement with your spouse, but I would highly encourage the friendship of another couple to partner with in this journey.
- **Give** - Don't think just because you're in debt means you can't afford to give. Often times giving is the key that unlocks more provision in our lives. One of my dearest friends in the

world graduated college with more than $115,000 in student loans. He and his wife were diligent to live on a plan, worked hard to pay off their debt, and within three years were completely debt free. However, the most powerful part of their story is that in addition to paying off their debt, they were also able to give tens of thousands of dollars away in the process. They had a family member do the math on how long it took them to pay off their debt and she said, "This just doesn't make sense. There is no way you guys should have been able to get out of debt this fast!" I wholeheartedly believe giving was the secret key that unlocked more provision for them and helped them get out of debt that much faster.

> IF WE ARE IN DEBT, WE SHOULD UNDERSTAND WHY WE'RE THERE AND DO WHATEVER IT TAKES TO GET OUT OF IT.

DEBT PAYOFF

Now that you have done the prep work, you are ready to get down to business! It is time to start attacking your debt with everything you have in you. In order to make sure you actually win this fight, we are going to teach a strategy that will help you become victorious no matter your debt load.

The method we teach has been taught by financial advisors for decades and is known as the debt snowball plan. With the debt snowball plan, the first step is to develop a Cash Flow Plan so you know where your money is going and how much you will have to work with to pay off the debt. In your CFP, be sure to include the minimum payments for all debts. Now, list your debt in order from smallest to largest. With any leftover money, you will put all of your extra money towards your smallest debt. We are not worrying about the interest rates unless the principal amounts are the same. This method is all about momentum. Once your first debt is eliminated, take the amount you were putting towards the first debt and add it to your minimum payment for the second debt. As you continue to pay off each debt you will then move on from your second debt to your third, fourth, fifth, and so on, until you are completely debt free!

GET THERE FASTER

So, you are committed to becoming debt free no matter what it takes and you are working on the debt snowball plan, but what are some secrets to helping you become debt free more quickly? Here are a few ways to help ignite the journey to debt freedom:

Work Extra

If you want to pay down your debt faster, it always helps to have more money! Pick up overtime or a part time job. Go sack groceries at the local grocery store, deliver pizzas, or work the night shift at a factory. One of my friends worked at an office where she could max out her overtime every week, so she would show up to work at six o'clock in the morning and work late in order to help them get out of debt quicker. Don't let your pride stop you from applying for the jobs that aren't glamorous or might seem too hard.

Sell Stuff

More breakthroughs happen for people when they finally decide to sell their cars. Not only are you able to unload thousands of dollars in debt, but it also gives you an extra $300 to $600 per month to use to pay down more of your other debt. Or if you don't have a car to sell, find things around the house you can sell. One of our friends didn't have many "extra" items, so he began asking all of his friends for things they wanted to give away. He collected their "throwaways" for a few weeks then held a garage sale and made close to $1,500!

Creatively Cut Expenses

We have more expenses in our lives than we realize that we could cut. Some of the obvious ones are cable, eating out, and shopping. But if you need to cut deeper into your expenses, you may have to come up with some creative ways. Here are some ideas from our classes: Car pool, locate closer to work, refinance the mortgage, make a monthly meal menu and only buy food for what's on the menu, make gifts for Christmas and birthdays, downsize your house, invite a younger person to live with your family and pay rent, cut meal portions in half, give up soft drinks for a year, have a "stay-cation", turn your thermostat higher or lower depending on season, and ride a bike to work. Obviously there are thousands of more ways to creatively cut expenses, but the point is that you can do anything for a short amount of time. You don't have to live this type of lifestyle forever, but it will more than likely help you realize which luxuries in life you can do without.

CHARLES' STORY REVISITED

It's unfortunate, but one of the most affective drivers for change is desperation. We can be as hopeful as we want, but unless that translates into doing whatever it takes to get debt free, it probably will not end up happening.

Charles and his wife were desperate for change. After years of making poor choices, they were ready for something different. They began the journey by getting on a budget. It was the first time in their marriage they actually knew how much money they had coming in and how much money they had going out. It helped them realize why they weren't getting anywhere. They were consistently overspending each month and didn't even know it! Recognition is the first step to transformation. Once they recognized where the money was going they were able to decide where they could make cuts to tackle the debt.

Charles decided he would need to work extra, so he began working a second job at a restaurant on nights and weekends. He also found odd-and-end jobs and, at one point, was working four jobs! Of course he was tired, but he knew he had to do something radical to get them out of the pit they were in.

As he brought in more income, they were able to pay off some of their smaller debts immediately, but it felt like they were barely making a dent in the mountain of debt, which was still over $100,000 at that time. Finally, one day they decided it was time to sell their beloved cars. Charles had a beautiful truck that he adored and was reluctant to sell. But once he made the move and got the cash, it gave him more energy and vision to keep knocking out even more debt. Looking back, Charles admits it was one of the hardest things he had ever done, but that one simple sacrifice freed up close to $1,000 per month.

Over the next few years he and his wife continued to make sacrifice after sacrifice. Whatever way they could trim back their lifestyle, they did it. In the span of four years, they were able to pay off over $80,000. Throughout this journey they have not had a very high income, but they have been faithful to do whatever it took to get debt free. When asked what his advice would be for people trying to get out of debt, Charles said this, "Don't let pride be a factor. Sometimes you may look silly or weird to everyone else around you, but your goal is different than theirs. You have to be okay taking on jobs below your pay-grade for a few years to give your family more peace for the next fifty years."

DON'T GO THERE

The best way to avoid the misery of being overleveraged and to putting yourself though a painful debt snowball plan is to do whatever it takes to stay out of debt in the first place. Truth is, most of us don't know how to manage debt and live within our means – we just don't know any better. No one ever taught us about the downfalls of debt and how difficult controlling it can be, so we walk straight into it without thinking twice. Life has a way of "catching up with us," but if we would simply take the time to plan, we could avoid overspending in areas we hadn't planned. Over-spending in one area causes strains and shortfalls and slowly creeps into every other area of our financial needs. Eventually we are forced to seek funds to fill in the gap and we typically do this by borrowing or overextending credit. Without doubt, the leading reason for debt is lack of contentment. To stay out of debt, our most powerful weapon is to learn the secret of contentment. When friends buy that big house or drive a really nice car, it can bring something up inside, compelling us to want the same thing. Just say, "NO." Stay focused and choose to be content with the provision God has given you.

> TO STAY OUT OF DEBT, OUR MOST POWERFUL WEAPON IS TO LEARN THE SECRET OF CONTENTMENT.

SAVE UP AN EMERGENCY FUND

We have talked about it before, but emergencies do happen. More emergencies happen than we expect, so we have to prepare ahead of time and save for them. Starting out, I suggest you save for a "starter fund" in the ballpark of $500 to $1,000. After that, depending upon our stage of life, volatility of our jobs and lifestyle habits, we should probably have a larger emergency fund ranging from two to nine months' worth of "bare bones expenses." These are going to be the basic expenses, which do not include eating out, retirement savings, extra clothing, etc. Remember, this is an emergency fund, not a mini-retirement fund. When Jenny and I first started saving for an emergency fund, we prayed and decided on a number we felt like fit our needs and our lifestyle at the time. Over the years, as we have added kids, cars, and responsibilities, we have increased that number.

If we consistently max out our lifestyle, spending our money without a plan, I guarantee we will have more emergencies than someone who is living on a plan. Emergencies might not be the transmission going out on the car or a major hospital bill, but instead our emergencies will be normal things like Christmas, birthdays, and back-to-school clothing! When we don't live on a plan, we are in a constant state of emergency because we are only looking at what we have to take care of today, instead of what is coming down the pike two weeks, two months or two years from now. As we develop a plan and live on it, we will get out of the "hand-to-mouth" lifestyle and no longer live paycheck to paycheck.

TRUST GOD TO PROVIDE

The most important way to avoid debt is to step out of the material world and put our trust in the God who knows exactly what we need. Not many people want to start with this one, but three-quarters of the items on this list are about us being responsible. Many times we believe that because God has not provided for us in the time and way we think He should, we take matters into our own hands and find provision for ourselves. When in reality,

God is standing there inviting us to trust Him and watch Him provide in a miraculous way.

GOD IS STANDING THERE INVITING US TO TRUST HIM AND WATCH HIM PROVIDE IN A MIRACULOUS WAY.

Several years ago I had a friend who wanted to go back and get his teacher's certification. He didn't have the money to pay for it and the certification bill was due in the next week. I talked with him and we prayed that God would provide and he committed to not take out a loan. The next day his dad called and said he had received a tax refund in the mail and he wanted to give it to him for the certification. It was within $3 of the amount he needed for the bill. If he hadn't trusted God and waited patiently, he would have missed out on a beautiful story and an experience in God's faithfulness and provision.

YOU CAN BE FREE

In the fall of 1849, a woman by the name of Harriet Tubman courageously stepped out into the unknown, leaving behind the only life she had ever known – decades of slavery. It was a dangerous decision that could easily have cost her life, but she knew the life she was living was no life at all. Over the next eight years, she became known as the conductor of the Underground Railroad and helped thousands of other slaves find their way to freedom. When asked about her heroic acts she had this to say, "I freed a thousand slaves, but I could have freed a thousand more if they would have only known they were slaves."[6]

In our culture, we have become convinced debt is just a normal part of life. Millions of people silently comply with this norm and live substandard lives because they don't know that there is another way. Let me tell you, there is better way. We don't have to constantly be overwhelmed by our credit card bill. We don't always have to have a car payment. We don't have to have student loans for the next twenty years! If we are currently in debt, there is a clear path out of it. If we are debt free currently – great! Let's stay debt free for the rest of our lives.

APPLICATION QUESTIONS

How has culture coerced you to believe debt is "okay" or it is the "only way"?

What are habits you need to consistently perform in order to ensure you don't go into debt?

What causes you to go into debt?

If you are currently in debt, what is the next step you need to take in order to begin the journey towards freedom?

CAPSTONE COURSE

I can hear it now, "What is a capstone course?" Glad you asked. As we close in this final chapter, it's important to consider how we want to finish. The capstone course is the culminating lesson in a course of study. In our case, this chapter will summarize all that we've learned about realigning our financial lives and free us to give like never before.

RICHEST MAN IN THE WORLD

In the early 1900's there lived a man by the name of John D. Rockefeller. This man was rich. Really, really rich. He was the first baron of the oil industry, and he is believed to be the wealthiest person in the history of the world. At one point during his lifetime, his net worth totaled more than $350 billion (in adjusted dollars).[1] Just to put that into context, Bill Gates is the second wealthiest person in the world currently and his net worth is a measly $75 billion. You could combine the net worth of Bill Gates and the next five wealthiest people in the world and John D. would still be wealthier than all of them combined![2] This guy had some cash.

After his death, reporters around the globe were groveling for a chance to find out exactly how much he was worth and what was going to happen to all of his money. During an interview with his personal accountant, a reporter finally posed the question, "So, how much did John D. leave behind?" The accountant looked around and thought about it for a minute, then answered, "He left ... *all* of it."[3] You see, John D. Rockefeller had accumulated extraordinary amounts of wealth in his lifetime, but just like the pauper down the street, he left every last penny here on this earth.

The same will be true for you. No matter how much money you make during your lifetime, when the final hour comes, you do not get to take any of it with you.

But ... you can make an incredible impact while you are here. And that impact will echo in eternity. The question then becomes, "What kind of impact do you want to have? Do you want a soft thud, or do you want a resounding boom!"

> WHEN THE FINAL HOUR COMES, YOU DO NOT GET TO TAKE ANY OF IT WITH YOU.

UNLOCKING THE POWER OF GIVING

Throughout the book we have talked about how God's purpose for our money and life is to know Him and make Him known. Through proper management of our resources, God wants us to come to a greater knowledge of Him and then allow others around the world to experience that same grace and truth. The problem is we rarely connect God's purpose with our daily realities. We tell ourselves, "Someday I will get to that." And the excuses feel very valid. There are more than enough worries for today, our responsibilities are overwhelming, and we feel ill-prepared to even consider accomplishing something more than just paying our bills and buying groceries.

We have outlined several practices that will help us realign our finances with God's way of doing things, but the capstone piece to all of this is the secret of *giving*. If we fail to remember to give, it would be like building a sports car, yet forgetting to put the engine in it! Giving is the force that allows our financial life to operate with power and intentionality, and it is the key to keeping our minds, hearts, and resources perpetually aligned with God's purposes.

Here are some keys to becoming an extravagant giver and participating in God's purposes for this world and your financial life: Start with the Tithe, Go on an Adventure, and Let it Flow.

START WITH THE TITHE

As we talk about giving in the context of Christian communities, we first need to start with the practice of giving a tithe, which simply means a "tenth." In the Old Testament tradition, the tithe was practiced by the children of Israel by bringing the first ten percent of their crops, livestock and/or produce to the local temple storehouse. This would then be used to provide for: the needs of the temple priests, the needs of those visiting (or strangers), and the needs of the orphans and widows.

Tithing has been given a black eye by some modern theologians who say the tithe is an Old Testament law and it no longer applies. But God implemented the principle of the tithe for the children of Israel, as well as for modern day believers for three main purposes: the tithe is a reminder of ownership, it helps us keep God first in our finances, and it solidifies trust as the foundation of our lives.

Reminder of Ownership

"A tithe of everything from the land, whether grain from the soil
or fruit from the trees, belongs to the Lord; it is holy to the Lord."
Leviticus 27:30

The tithe serves as a consistent reminder of who the real owner is. In the ancient world, it was a common practice. Landowners would collect a ten percent ownership fee from those who used the land. Psalms 23:1 says, "The earth is the LORD's and the fullness thereof ..." (ESV). Therefore, we are hard-pressed to see this as anything other than God implying the principle of the tithe. He was doing so to remind them He was the owner of everything. He has yet given up ownership; therefore His invitation still stands as a way to acknowledge it in our financial lives through the tithe.

Keeps God First

"And before the LORD your God, in the place that he
will choose, to make his name dwell there, you shall eat the tithe
of your grain, of your wine, and of your oil, and the
firstborn of your herd and flock, that you may learn to
fear the LORD your God always."
Deuteronomy 14:23 (ESV)

Secondly, the tithe allows us to keep giving as a normal part of our everyday lives so we do not become too introspective and selfish. With the tithe as the first expense, it forces us to remember that life is about God and others first. The tithe is a place of worship and right alignment as it helps keep us focused on the first priority in our lives. God exhorts us and commands us to give the tithe, because He understands in His wisdom and kindness, our lives function better when He is first.

GOD'S PURPOSE FOR OUR MONEY AND LIFE IS TO KNOW HIM AND MAKE HIM KNOWN.

Trust as the Foundation

"The LORD said to Moses, 'Consecrate to me every first-born male. The first offspring of every womb among the Israelites belongs to me, whether human or animal.'"

Exodus 13:1-2

Third, the tithe forces us to keep trust as the foundation of our financial stories. At its core, the tithe is built on trust. As we give the tithe we are committing to give God the first and best, and then trusting Him with the rest. In Biblical times, resources were not cash and coins; but produce, livestock, and crops. When that first little lamb was born, and God asked the shepherd to give it as a first fruit, the shepherd trusted God that He would provide more. God has implemented the tithe so our trust would not be in our resources or our wealth, but instead in Him.

Pre-Law, Post-Law or In-Law?

Many times, I am asked if the "principle of the tithe" is only applicable to the Old Testament because we are no longer under Jewish law. This is a valid question, but if we look closely, we will see the principle of the tithe is given before the Jewish Law and after the Law is fulfilled in the person of Jesus.

In the book of Genesis, we see where Abram gave a tithe of his earnings from victory to a figure named Melchizedek.[3] The principle of the tithe was alive and well hundreds of years before the "law" of the tithe was given to the children of Israel.

And if we flip to the New Testament, we see a great example of how the principle is actually post-law and is still applicable even in this new era of grace.

> "Woe to you, teachers of the law and Pharisees, you hypo-
> crites! You give a tenth of your spices – mint, dill and cum-
> in. But you have neglected the more important matters of
> the law – justice, mercy and faithfulness. You should have
> practiced the latter, without neglecting the former."
> Matthew 23:23

Many will quote this verse as Jesus' teaching against the practice of giving a tithe, however it's the exact opposite as He says, "You should have practiced the latter, without neglecting the former." Jesus is not lowering the bar on our giving; He is taking it to an even higher level. We see this as a common theme throughout all of His teachings. He attacks the practice of simply checking off boxes and "looking" religious, and calls us to a higher level of living in grace. Jesus affirms the Old Testament laws about not killing or committing adultery, while also calling us to purify our hearts and minds and not simply our actions.[4] Jesus' teachings are radical and call us to greater dependency upon Him. So the argument can easily be made that He is raising the bar on giving and inviting us to be open-handed with all we have. Ultimately, the "law" of the tithe is not the issue at stake. It is a question of ownership and our recognition that it all belongs to God.

THE TITHE HELPS US GET GOING IN THE RIGHT DIRECTION, BUT IT WAS NEVER INTENDED TO BE THE STOPPING POINT FOR OUR LIFE OF GIVING.

Training Wheels

"Bring the whole tithe into the storehouse, that there may be food in my house. Test me in this,' says the LORD almighty, 'and see if I will not throw open the floodgates of heaven and pour out so much blessing that there will not be room enough to store it.'"

Malachi 3:10

This last year I was meeting with a friend who shared about his family's financial struggles. He was in a tough spot with his job and their finances were not adding up. They had been trying to pay down debt, but recently just felt stuck. We went through every area of their finances, and even I couldn't figure out what was going on. Finally, I graciously asked him if they were giving a tithe. He said they were giving, but it was probably in the range of two to three percent and was not as regular as he liked. I showed him how God invites us to test him with the tithe in Malachi 3 and then encouraged him to work towards getting to ten percent. He committed to the process and admitted to being scared and afraid everything would fall apart. What happened over the next few months was pretty amazing.

He and his wife made a budget and committed to start giving a tithe as their first expense. He would literally drive to the church on payday and write out a check to make sure that it was the "first fruit." On paper it didn't look like it would work, but over the next few months it was like the floodgates were opened up. He was given an even better job than the one he applied for and he was consistently given opportunities to make more money. He and his wife paid off more debt in a few short months than they had the entire previous year. The most powerful part about their story is that for the first time in their twelve years of marriage, they were able to pay all of their bills at the beginning of the month. But you know what else happened? He and his wife became addicted to giving and they actually began giving over and above the tithe for the first time ever. Even in the midst of their need, they realized God wanted to take them on a great adventure, and they knew He would provide for them along the way.

My friends had experienced the power of Malachi 3 coming to fruition in their lives. As they chose to step out and trust God with their ten percent tithe, God was faithful to meet them.

Giving for believers always starts with the tithe. Oftentimes, we set the tithe as the ultimate goal of our giving, when in fact it is simply the starting point for a lifestyle of giving extravagantly. Randy Alcorn refers to the tithe as "the training wheels for a life of giving."[5] The tithe helps us get going in the right direction, but it was never intended to be the stopping point for our life of giving.

GO ON AN ADVENTURE!

An important key to extravagant giving is a willingness to go on an adventure with God. If you've been in a church for any amount of time, it is almost certain you have heard a verse quoted as the tithe and offerings buckets were passed around. In the second book of Corinthians, Paul encourages the church in Corinth that "Each of you should give what you have decided in your heart to give, not reluctantly or under compulsion, for God loves a cheerful giver."[6] Doesn't that sound so sweet? God loves it when we give our money away with a smile. Well, for me personally, it's usually not that easy. I don't want to give my money away. I'm selfish and I want to keep it! Honestly, I have hated that verse. I know it's not right to hate scripture, so maybe I should say I have hated how that verse has been used to manipulate people either into giving or not giving. It would get so bad that if I heard someone quote this verse I would immediately shut my brain off and wait for the closing prayer.

I studied the meaning of this phrase in the Greek and my attitude changed immediately. I first took a look at the word "cheerful." When translated, this word is actually "willing."[7] And this makes sense because Paul is encouraging the Corinthian church to not give under compulsion, but to give "willingly." However, the real "aha" moment came when I studied the meaning of the word "giver." It looks straightforward on the surface, but as I unpacked it in more detail I discovered it is not a onetime act, but a lifestyle. The word "to give" can be translated as "to go on an adventure."[8] Now that is something I can get excited about! This verse on the surface can appear to say God just wants someone to give Him money and do it all with a smile on their face. Lame! What God is really looking for is "Someone who is willing to go on an adventure!"

This helped me realize God doesn't want our money or care if we give to Him or to His church. His call is for someone who will look beyond selfish desires and say "yes" to whatever He's asking. He wants someone who is willing to give everything away and partner with Him in His redemptive plan. God is not looking for a robot with a comb-over and pocket-protector that can responsibly check off another box on their "Good Christian To-

Do List." He is in the business of recruiting men and women who will jump up off of the couch and run out the door to explore the adventure He has in process. More than hoping you will be a happy giver who regularly puts twenty bucks in the offering plate, God is after your heart. He wants someone who is willing to go on an adventure.

> **WHAT GOD IS REALLY LOOKING FOR IS "SOMEONE WHO IS WILLING TO GO ON AN ADVENTURE!"**

Balloons

When Jenny was eight months pregnant with our oldest son, Asher, we learned a valuable lesson in going on an adventure with God. At that point in our lives, we didn't have a lot of discretionary income. We were doing our best to plan, save, and give, but within a matter of days our financial life felt like it was unraveling. At the beginning of the week, we sat down to do our monthly Cash Flow Plan and after a few simple calculations, we quickly realized we were several hundred dollars short for the month. A couple days later, I called the insurance company and received some bad news. We had been saving months for our hospital bills for the birth, but the insurance company told me we actually needed to have double the amount we had saved. The next day I was backing out of our driveway and heard a loud "Pop." I jumped out of the car just in time to watch our front tire go flat from a nail. I couldn't take it anymore.

I ran inside and Jenny and I just wept together. It felt like the whole world was against us and we could not catch a break. We sat down and prayed, asking God what we needed to do. I was more than willing to go out and mow some yards or pick up another job. But as we prayed, we both sensed God asking us to just trust Him. That night we went to our small group and it just so happened to be a night we were all giving to someone in need. But of course, that week we were giving to someone else! Our group spent some time praying as couples and deciding what amount we should give to our friend. Jenny and I looked at each other and mouthed, "ARE YOU KIDDING ME?" We both prayed heartless prayers, hoping God would just say, "Hey guys, it's okay. You can just take a break tonight." But in God's beautiful sense of humor, we both felt like He was asking us to give $300 to our friend.

Here we were already several hundred dollars in the hole, with several thousand dollars coming due in the next month, and a tire that needed to be replaced, and we were being invited to give! At that moment, we were not "cheerful," but we were "willing to go on an adventure." With all the joy we could muster up from our empty tank, we wrote a check for $300 and gave it to our friend, and wondered how in the world we were going to make it that month.

That night, after small group, we went to the grocery store to pick up a few things. When we came home we noticed there were some balloons on our front door knob. In perfect eight-month pregnant woman fashion, Jenny huffed and said, "I'm really not in the mood for balloons right now." But as we got a little bit closer to the balloons, we noticed there was something inside of them. We took the balloons inside and began to pop them and out of each balloon fell large bills – $20's and $50's, and even a couple of $100's. Balloon after balloon was filled with cash. By the time we popped the last balloon, our entire floor was covered in hundreds of dollars of cash. Enough money to cover the amount we had given that night, our blown tire, and the deficit in our budget. We hadn't told anyone about our situation, but God knew, and He knew where we lived. And to top it off, after the delivery of our baby, we received a bill from the hospital and it was a fraction of the amount our insurance company had told us it would be.

God desires people who will say "yes" to an adventure with Him. He wants us to trust Him with our lives and finances in order to see the world changed. It might be painful, or it might be treacherous. But you never know, it could even be a little fun. Either way, I guarantee there is more joy when we go on an adventure with God than there is sitting on our couch and keeping all our money in our pockets.

LET IT FLOW

The principle of giving is to keep the money moving. God created us to have hearts and lives that are fully alive when we facilitate this movement. There are two well-known bodies of water that best exemplify the different paths our financial stories can take.

The first is the Colorado River, which starts high in the Rocky Mountains near the Continental Divide. If we were standing on top of where this river begins, we probably wouldn't even know we were there. It starts as a tiny puddle that bubbles out of the ground and slowly trickles down the side of the mountain. Humble and insignificant as it continues to flow, other streams connect and join the torrent, as it eventually becomes a mighty river. The river travels through Colorado, into Utah, down into Arizona and Nevada, into California, and finally makes its way into Mexico. What once seemed like a trivial puddle welling up from the ground ends up traveling over 1,450 miles, and along its path brings life to more than thirty million people. In addition, the Colorado provides power to the Hoover Dam, which gives light and electricity to more than seven states.

On the other hand, there is another body of water with a different fate. The Jordan River is a major waterway in the Middle East that travels 150 miles and empties into a body of water called the Dead Sea. This sea has a similar amount of water as the Colorado River, but it has one clear distinction – it doesn't flow out. All of the water wandering the Jordan River stops at the Dead Sea, making it one of the saltiest bodies of water in the world. It has the same amount of water and potential as the Colorado River; however it fails to support any life – plants, animals or people.

The picture is clear. We have been entrusted with resources to manage, and God has created us to keep it flowing, bringing life to those in need. He has put dreams inside of our hearts and wants to bring His life, light, and healing to millions of people, and that can only be accomplished if we partner with Him by allowing our money to flow.

It might not *feel* like you have a lot of money and in reality, you actually might not have tons of wealth. However, just like the Colorado River, beginning as an insignificant puddle, it still brings life and healing to more than thirty million people and seven states. God can take your resources, whether much or little, and bring life and healing to millions around the world as you allow it to flow.

What Could We Do?

We began this book with the story of my friend who had reached the top of the ladder and was left empty and miserable. If I were to end this book by telling you to just go out and buy cars with your cash and do whatever else you want, as long as you stick to a Cash Flow Plan, I would be leading you up that same ladder. If the horizon of our financial stories is simply wealth creation, we will eventually become burnt out, disinterested and unfulfilled. Let's consider rewriting our stories, realigning our priorities to discover what we can do with our money that would echo in eternity.

Currently the average American household spends roughly $1,000 per month on debt payments, not including home mortgage.[9] But more than just debt payments, we spend tens of thousands of dollars each year on frivolous things that don't have an impact. I believe there are literally billions of dollars tied up that God wants to release. What could we do if we allowed just a little bit of this money to be used for a better cause?

Here are just a few ideas to get us thinking, but there are many more. By partnering with International Justice Mission, for $4,500[10] you can help one woman be set free from sex trafficking. It costs about $30 to support one orphan per month ($360/year) through Compassion International.[11] And through Living Water International, you can provide clean water for one person for as little as $1 per year.[12]

What could you do if you were not spending $1,000 on debt payments or other things each month?

Women Freed	# _____
Orphans Sponsored	# _____
People with Clean Water	# _____

You could rescue three women from sex trafficking each year, support more than thirty orphans per month, or give clean water to more than 12,000 thirsty people. All within one year – amazing! You can do a whole lot, but only if you free up your resources and let them flow.

Maybe you are a part of a local church. Let's take a look at what your church could do if every single person was free from that $1,000 per month. If your church had only one hundred families, you would be spending $100,000 on debt or other things every single month! Calculate the effect that could be made based on the number of families in your church.

Women Freed	#	_____
Orphans Sponsored	#	_____
People with Clean Water	#	_____

If everyone in your church had no debt, you could free more than 260 women from sex trafficking each year, or you could support more than 3,300 orphans per month, or you could provide clean water to more than 1.2 million people, which is the entire country of Swaziland! Every single year, a church of one hundred families can literally provide clean water to a new country that is desperately in need of it.

The Great Potential

The potential is endless for what we could do with our resources – *if* we released them for their proper purpose. I am certain it can happen. If each person decided to take responsibility for his or her financial life by restoring beliefs, realigning plans, remaining focused and giving generously, we could literally change the world. Imagine!

THE POTENTIAL IS ENDLESS FOR WHAT WE COULD DO WITH OUR RESOURCES – IF WE RELEASED THEM FOR THEIR PROPER PURPOSE.

PULLING IT ALL TOGETHER

Last February Jenny and I taught the *REALIGN* class in Seattle. At the end of our session, a guy named Jared approached us and said that he and his wife had felt called overseas, but were in the middle of paying off close to $75,000 in debt and just didn't think it was possible.

We prayed for them and encouraged them to keep working hard. But, when we finished praying, he commented that he felt like God told him that they would be debt free by the end of April (three months away).

April 29th rolled around and Jared had been working over one hundred hours each week and complaining to God about how tired he was. He just didn't think they would be debt free by the end of the month since they still had $14,000 to go and only one day to get there. The next day the church called him up and told him to come get an envelope that someone anonymously just dropped off for them – it was cash and too much money to keep at the church. After counting it all up, it was $15,000! They were completely debt free by the end of April, just like God said!

Amazing, right? But it gets better. Shortly after they became debt free Jared ended up breaking his ankle. They didn't have health insurance because he was planning on getting it once they were debt free. The bill was $30,000 and they just didn't have it, so he wrote a letter to the hospital asking for financial assistance. With all the money he had been making from his hard work to pay off his debts, the hospital declined assistance because he had been making too much.

At the same time, Jared had been working on a home remodel owned by one of the surgeons at the hospital he owed. The surgeon ended up calling the hospital manager and told him to give them some kind of financial assistance. He said, "You guys write off bills all the time for people who will continue to be a drain on society, and this guy and his wife are actually doing something great!" The next week my friend got a letter in the mail telling him that he had 100% financial assistance!

Jared and his wife realigned their thinking with what God said, and are now overseas in the mission field. They are pursuing their "God-given" dream, but they worked incredibly hard and with incredible faith to get there.

The ultimate goal of realigning your financial life is not that you have enough stuff and have no debt, but we want you to be free so you can say "yes" to whatever God is inviting you to. He is doing incredible things around the world and is looking for people who will seek first His Kingdom and realign their financial lives to accomplish His purposes. The journey to get there may not be easy, but it will be worth it. Whatever your dream, the power to bring healing and a little bit of heaven to our broken world is literally in your hands. Let it flow.

APPLICATION QUESTION

When you think about the type of impact that you want to have in this world, what would be something that you'd like your money to accomplish?

What are some of the things that keep you from opening your hands and being willing to give?

What can you do today to take the first step towards going on an adventure with God?

THE REALIGN STORY

Sometimes in life you end up doing things you thought you'd never do. In my case, I didn't think I'd be working in full-time ministry. Yet, in January of 2008, I found myself sitting at a kitchen table with a friend and planning out a new financial ministry to help people navigate their way out of the trappings of debt and poor financial decisions. Talk about a complete 180-degree turnaround!

What caught my attention was how there seemed to be a natural connection between people's financial wreckage and their spiritual brokenness. As people learned Christian precepts for restoring their finances, they also experienced restoration in their relationship with God. I decided to quit my job as an insurance salesman and launched a new venture with great hopes and dreams ... but no money! The next two months I lived off of my savings and had zero income. To make the situation a little more complicated, I was engaged to be married within a few short months, but, thankfully, my bride-to-be and in-laws were supportive.

In order to launch our non-profit, we established a board consisting of several key staff members and business leaders from our church. Our pastor, Jimmy Seibert, had heard about our ministry and let me know that he loved what we were doing. He said he would like to see the local church own the task of financial restoration. We all agreed that it would be best to bring our ministry operations under the covering of our local church, Antioch Community Church.

A few short weeks after that conversation, I married the girl of my dreams and one week later started my new job as Director of the Financial Restoration Ministry at Antioch. I was a "seasoned" twenty-three year old.

LAUNCHED OUT

That fall, after meeting with dozens of families for financial counseling, we decided to host a financial equipping class to reach a larger audience. I was hoping we would have five to ten people attend the first class, but we had more than seventy people present, representing forty-two households and consisting of recent college graduates all the way to couples who had been married for thirty years.

Prior to launching the class, we took a survey to determine the needs of those who would be attending. We discovered that over 75 percent of our members regularly gave ten percent of their income to the local church. For all intents and purposes, we believed our church body was financially healthy. If they were giving and supporting the work of the church, we assumed they didn't have financial problems. However, during the first class, we had each household write down their total debt load, not including home mortgage or business debt. Of forty-two households represented, they had a total debt load of $1.1 million dollars. That's an average of over $26,000 per household. Wow, that completely shocked us.

I can vividly remember taking those 3x5 cards into my office to tally the numbers, and as I flipped through each card I was overwhelmed by the magnitude of the financial wreckage in so many people's lives. Over the next few years our team of facilitators and financial coaches had the honor of educating thousands in our classes, as well as meeting one-on-one for financial coaching.

A NEED FOR A CHANGE

Fast forward a few years and we have seen incredible results from these classes. There are also some lessons learned along the way that are worth noting. The first is we discovered that many of the problems people have with their finances are related to their desire to live the "American Dream," often to the exclusion of what God might intend for them to do with their resources. As a consequence we incorporated a Biblical and eternal perspective into the teachings. We focused on the importance of living for God's Kingdom and being generous through the entire journey.

Another lesson learned came when we were approached by one of our international churches to help them find a financial curriculum. I soon realized the teachings wouldn't translate to other cultures. Not just the practical issues of mortgages and insurances, but the very state of mind and belief system that we were communicating. It was all very ... "American." We would teach that if you worked hard, stayed out of debt and were generous, then you would be "financially successful." But when you are sitting in the dirt talking with a mom who is cooking balls of rice for her babies and making $1 a day, those formulas fly out the window. This mom worked harder in one day than I did all year. She wasn't in debt and her depth of generosity embarrasses me.

Finally, I realized we weren't *truly* setting people free financially. We were simply getting them out of debt and helping them earn more money so they could just go buy all they wanted with cash instead of credit cards. We were missing the whole point. The real goal was to set people free from the *love of money and the slavery of the envy, greed, and constant comparison,* so they could pursue God's Kingdom.

Sure people had a more positive financial balance sheet, but we were not dealing with the underlying issues that caused the problems in the first place. Greed, discontentment, lack of trust in God, and an unwillingness to living open-handed were all major issues that Jesus talked about, but were being omitted from the teachings.

BACK TO THE BEGINNING

I was extremely frustrated by this. I thought to myself, "If our teachings don't translate to other countries and contexts, and peoples' hearts aren't set free, then are we really basing them on Biblical principles?" The teachings in the Bible, after all, were created before America even existed. I grabbed a notepad and went outside and sat down on a picnic table and processed my thoughts with God. After several minutes, going around and around with Him, I felt like He gave me a very simple answer, "Josh, in order to understand My perspective and My purposes for finances go back to the beginning."

So I flipped open my Bible to the very beginning and began reading something I had read one hundred times before – the Creation story in Genesis. As I read, it was like I was seeing the scripture for the very first time. It sounded so simple, but I finally realized that God's original purpose for our money is to know Him and make Him known. Alright, but "How do we do this?" I read all the way through chapter four and at the end I thought I had something. I picked up some stones from the ground below me and then scribbled on my paper – "God's big financial rocks: live for God's Kingdom first, believe truth, manage God's resources, and be content with what you've been given." These rocks were the foundational truths that started in the Garden and were weaved throughout Scripture. If these foundational principles were indeed truths, they could stand the test of time and cross over racial, economic, and cultural boundaries.

TESTING THE TRUTHS

From that time on, I began to unpack what I believe was God's original purpose for finances and how we are to align our lives to it. My team and I did our best to remove from the class anything that seemed too American, or didn't translate to people in different economic situations.

It was now time to put our approach to the test. If we could teach them successfully to the poorest in our city, then these principles could be taught almost anywhere. So, we decided to teach the class at the local Salvation Army to a group of transitioning ex-felons. The material was received extremely well and people's lives were changed. However, the next class would be the biggest stretch of all.

Our church, Antioch Community Church, has been starting new churches around the world since the early 1990's. One of the first churches we planted was in Irkutsk, Russia, which is in Southern Siberia. The executive pastor at the church had recently emailed me to ask if we had any financial curriculum they could use. I sent them what we had and within a few months they had translated the class material into Russian and taught it to their entire church twice! They emailed me back and expressed that they could not believe how successful the class had been. From the ex-drug addict to the budding entrepreneur, the class impacted each of them and brought Biblical truths to their specific situation.

This book follows the transforming principles taught in our *REALIGN* financial curriculum, which will completely change your perspective. We can try to solve the surface level problems of debt, stress and money fights. But in order to see lasting change, we must address these problems from the inside out. I have witnessed countless people set free – people who were trapped in the rat race, with a mountain of debt, and fighting a losing battle. My hope and prayer is that you join the growing numbers of those set free.

ACKNOWLEDGEMENTS

To God: It seems trite to give a simple tip of the cap to my Creator and Sustainer, but it is only through You that I would have a story to tell in the first place. Thank you for paying the greatest price of Your life to bring my life into realignment. You saw me when I was in darkness and called me by a new name and marked Your love upon my heart.

To My Beautiful Bride: We know who the hero is.

To My Boys: Your smiles and tickle fights are the only rewards this daddy will ever need. Stay happy, stay focused, stay free.

To the Antioch Movement: This book is your breath and song. You deserve the credit for living these truths out for decades, and I am simply a recipient of your faithfulness to God.

To the Clear Day Team: Thank you for believing in us through this process and continuing to put your shoulder into every part of it.

To Mom and Dad: Thanks for trying for "one more." Momma, thank you for praying me through. Dad, thank you for making me a man.

NOTES

Introduction – Fellowship of the Broken/Ladder on the Right Wall
1 - Gen. 3:12
2 - Gen. 3:7
3 - Gen. 3:21
4 - Rom. 5:18
5 - Eph. 4:22-24
6 - Covey, Stephen R. *The 7 Habits of Highly Effective People: Restoring the Character Ethic.* New York: Free Press, 2004.
7 - Matt. 23:25-26
8 - Matt. 6:33 (ESV)
9 - Thomas, Gary L. *Sacred Marriage: The Greatest Challenge in the World.* Zondervan, 2000. 13.
10 - Gen. 12:1-3
11 - Matt. 6:9-10 (ESV)

Chapter 1 – Roots Before Fruits
1 - Erikson, Erik H. *Childhood and Society.* New York: W.W. Norton & Company, 1963.
2 - Matt. 7:16-18

Chapter 2 – Lies That Drive
1 - DeSilva, Stephen K. *Money and the Prosperous Soul: Tipping the Scales of Favor and Blessing.* Grand Rapids, MI: Chosen Books, 2010.
2 - Olsen, Christoper M. "Natural Rewards, Neuroplasticity, and Non-drug Addictions." *Neuropharmacology* 61 (2011): 1109-122.
3 - Rom. 12:2

4 - Cloud, Dr. Henry. *The Law of Happiness: How Spiritual Wisdom and Modern Science Can Change Your Life.* New York: Howard Books, 2011. 36.

5 - Eph. 4:29 (ESV)

Chapter 3 – Change Your Mind

1 - Gen. 3:11

Chapter 4 – Money Made Simple

1 - Foster, Richard J. *Celebration of Discipline: The Path to Spiritual Growth.* Rev. 1st ed. San Francisco: Harper & Row, 1988.

2 - DeSilva, Stephen K. *Money and the Prosperous Soul: Tipping the Scales of Favor and Blessing.* Grand Rapids, MI: Chosen Books, 2010.

3 - Matt. 6:10

4 - Ps. 119:105

5 - Dijksterhuis, E. J. *Archimedes.* Princeton, N.J.: Princeton University Press, 1987. 15.

Chapter 6 – Managing Cash Flow

1 - "Job Switching." *I Love Lucy.* CBS. 30 May 1952. Television.

2 - Mint. https://www.mint.com/.

3 - You Need A Budget. http://www.youneedabudget.com/.

4 - REALIGN Class. http://www.realignclass.com/forms.html.

5 - REALIGN Class. http://www.realignclass.com/forms.html.

6 - SmartyPig. https://www.smartypig.com.

Chapter 8 – Throw Faith in the Mix

1 - Matt. 14:13-21

Chapter 9 – Always a Bigger Boat

1 - Eccl. 2:1, 4-8, 9-11 (ESV)

2 - Gen. 3:1

3 - Cloud, *The Law of Happiness*, 6.

4 - Cloud, *The Law of Happiness*, 102.

5 - I Thess. 5:18

6 - Greek philosopher (341 BC - 270 BC)

7 - Mischel, Walter, Ebbe B. Ebbesen, and Antonette Raskoff Zeiss. "Cognitive and Attentional Mechanisms in Delay of Gratification." *Journal of Personality and Social Psychology* 21, no. 2 (1972): 204-18.

Chapter 10 – Destructive Debt Story

1 - "Student Debt Levels – Now Averaging More Than $35,000 – Surprise To Half Of 2013 College Grads." Fidelity. January 1, 2013. http://www.fidelity.com/inside-fidelity/individual-investing/college-grads-surprised-by-student-debt-level-exceeds-35000.

2 - Holmes, Tamara E., and Yasmin Ghahremani. "Credit Card Debt Statistics." Creditcards.com. http://www.creditcards.com/credit-card-news/credit-card-debt-statistics-1276.php.

3 - "What's in My FICO Score." Myfico.com. http://www.myfico.com/crediteducation/whatsinyourscore.aspx.

4 - Prelec, Drazen, and Duncan Simester. "Always Leave Home Without It: A Further Investigation of the Credit-Card Effect on Willingness to Pay." *Marketing Letters* 12, no. 1 (2001): 5-12.

5 - Based upon average new car purchase price of $25,000.

6 - "Harriet Tubman Quotes." Goodreads.com. http://www.goodreads.com/author/quotes/59710.Harriet_Tubman.

Chapter 11 – Capstone Course

1 - Warner, Brian. "The 25 Richest People Who Ever Lived – Inflation Adjusted." Celebrity Net Worth. April 14, 2014. http://www.celebritynetworth.com/articles/entertainment-articles/25-richest-people-lived-inflation-adjusted/.

2 - Dolan, Kerry A., and Luisa Kroll. "Inside the 2014 Forbes Billionaires List: Facts and Figures." Forbes. March 3, 2014. http://www.forbes.com/sites/luisakroll/2014/03/03/inside-the-2014-forbes-billionaires-list-facts-and-figures/.

3 - Gen. 14:20

4 - Matt. 5:21-28

5 - Alcorn, Randy. *The Treasure Principle: Unlocking the Secret of Joyful Giving.* New York: Multnomah Books, 2001. 17-18.

6 - 2 Cor. 9:7

7 - Strong, James. *The New Strong's Exhaustive Concordance of the Bible: With Main Concordance, Appendix to the Main Concordance, Key Verse Comparison Chart, Dictionary of the Hebrew Bible, Dictionary of the Greek Testament.* Nashville: Thomas Nelson, 1984.

8 - Strong, James. *The New Strong's Exhaustive Concordance of the Bible.* 1984.

9 - Calculation of $1,000 per month debt payments based upon the current average student loan debt of approximately $30,000+ paid off over 10 years at 7% interest = $350 per month; combined with average car payment of $450+ per month; and average credit card debt of $7,000 = approximately $200 per month.

10 - International Justice Mission. https://www.ijm.org/.

11 - Compassion International. http://www.compassion.com/.

12 - Living Water International. http://www.water.cc

ABOUT THE AUTHOR

Josh Lawson created REALIGN with a passion to see people's identity, purpose and relationships restored by realigning their hearts to God's plan for their finances. REALIGN classes have been taught to businesses, non-profits, and churches around the world. Josh currently serves as Director of Community Engagement at Antioch Community Church in Waco, Texas, where he oversees the Financial Restoration Ministry and Impact Waco – the local holistic transformation branch of Antioch. He is the author of *Don't Get Suckered: How to Survive College Debt Free ... and with Your Shirt.* Josh and his wife Jenny currently reside in Waco, Texas, where they raise their two boys, Asher and Jack.

FOREWORD BY **MAX LUCADO**

PASSION & PURPOSE

BELIEVING THE CHURCH CAN
STILL CHANGE THE WORLD

JIMMY SEIBERT

MORE THAN ANOTHER FINANCIAL COURSE

A BRAND NEW & DIFFERENT FINANCIAL CURRICULUM

REALIGN focuses not only on the "nuts and bolts" of financial planning, but also emphasizes the spiritual aspects of money matters. REALIGN deals with the whole person, from the inside out, not simply finances. The power of this 8 week course is found in the fact that God is brought into every decision a person makes. The goal: to give every person a closer walk with God by allowing Him into financial decisions.

REALIGNCLASS.COM

WEBSITE: REALIGNCLASS.COM

TWITTER: @JOSHVLAWSON

EMAIL: INFO@REALIGNCLASS.COM